I0120725

R. C. Benton

# The Vermont settlers and the New York land speculators

R. C. Benton

**The Vermont settlers and the New York land speculators**

ISBN/EAN: 9783741146657

Manufactured in Europe, USA, Canada, Australia, Japa

Cover: Foto ©Thomas Meinert / pixelio.de

Manufactured and distributed by brebook publishing software
(www.brebook.com)

R. C. Benton

**The Vermont settlers and the New York land speculators**

# The Vermont Settlers

## AND THE

## New York Land Speculators.

R. C. BENTON.

# THE

# VERMONT SETTLERS

## AND THE

# NEW YORK LAND SPECULATORS

BY

DISTRIBUTED WITH COMPLIMENTS

OF THE AUTHOR.

# CONTENTS.

CONTENTS.

# THE

# VERMONT SETTLERS

# NEW YORK LAND SPECULATORS.

## CHAPTER I.

### EARLY MILITARY OUTPOSTS AND EXPLORATIONS.

The settlement of the territory now known as the state of Vermont was for a long time delayed by the continuance of the wars between France and England which followed the English Revolution of 1688. Until the close of the French and Indian Wars and the conquest of Canada in 1760, most of that territory was the pathway of the hostiles. The intervals of peace were not long enough to permit any permanent settlements beyond the protection of forts and garrisons. It is true that the settlements within the province of Massachusetts had extended up the valley of the Connecticut river, so that as early as 1724 a block house or fort was constructed near what is now the village of Brattleboro. Within a few years afterwards these outposts had been extended as far north as Number Four, now known as

Charlestown, New Hampshire; and around these block
houses a few settlers had ventured. But these were
simply military outposts or the advance guard of the
settlements in Massachusetts.

There had been also early occupation by the French
of grounds near Lake Champlain. The researches of
Mr. David Read, found in volumes one and two of
Miss Hemenway's Vermont Gazetteer, have shown
pretty clearly that a French fort was built on Isle La
Motte as early as 1666. At some considerable time
previous to the overthrow of the French power, other
French settlements were made on Windmill Point in
Alburg, on the Missisquoi river in Swanton, in Colchester near the mouths of the Lamoille and Winooski
rivers, and on Chimney Point in Addison. Judge
Strong, the historian of Addison, has also shown that
in 1690 a scouting party under the command of a Capt.
D' Narm, sent out by the Governor of New York, built
what was called a stone fort on Chimney Point, but it
does not appear that there was at that time anything
like a permanent settlement there. All these were,
however, only appendages of the outposts made necessary by the military occupation of the country. It is
safe to say that there was no settlement in what is now
Vermont, independent of its military occupation, until
after 1760.

The settlement of the new territory was especially
promoted by an occurrence near the close of that war.
It will be remembered that in September, 1759, at the
very time when Wolfe was making his final assault on
Quebec, Major Rogers started from Crown Point for a
raid on the St. Francis indians in Canada. He reached
their village on the 5th of October and inflicted upon

them the most serious punishment known in the indian
wars of this country. In fact, he destroyed the
power of those indians and completely took away
their courage. Although in 1752, during the short
interval of peace between the two last French and
Indian wars, they had sent messengers to the post at
Number Four, forbidding in arrogant terms the establishment of any English settlements on the great
meadows at Newbury and Haverhill, nevertheless,
when the upper Connecticut valley was settled some
ten years later, these St. Francis indians were found to
be the most peaceable and subdued indian tribes in any
of the American settlements.

The progress of the French and Indian wars gave
large opportunity for the people of New England to
get acquainted with this unexplored territory. In the
preceding wars there had been a few scouting parties
across some parts of the state, and some captives had
been dragged through its valleys, but there had been
no considerable explorations of that territory. Capt.
John Stark had in 1752 been taken prisoner by the
indians in northern New Hampshire, and had been
taken through the upper valley of the Connecticut,
which he described as an unknown country. After his
release, two years later, he conducted an exploring
party up the valley as far as Lancaster.

At the commencement of the war in 1755 troops
from New Hampshire and Massachusetts, in order to
reach Lake George and Ticonderoga, were obliged to
go around by way of Albany; but a party of Massachusetts soldiers, who had been at Lake George, in
making a short cut off for their homes, found the land
that they afterwards settled as the Town of Bennington.

During the next two or three campaigns, while the active hostilities were confined within the vicinity of Lake George and Ticonderoga, the scouting parties of the colonists, chief among which were Major Rogers with his rangers,—John Stark and others,—had made pretty thorough exploration of the whole of the present state, as well as of a portion of Canada.

It was, however, the campaign of 1759 that gave the best opportunity for the men of New England to become acquainted with the unsettled territory of Vermont. While Wolfe and Montcalm were girding themselves for their final struggle at Quebec, the English commander in chief, Sir Jeffrey Amherst, upon getting possession of Ticonderoga and Crown Point in the early summer, halted his army at a safe distance from the enemy and began the enormous but useless task of constructing a great fortress at Crown Point. Before the season closed, he had with him five thousand men from Connecticut under General Phinehas Lyman, and also militia men from Massachusetts and Rhode Island. During that season and the next a large force of New Hampshire men were engaged in constructing a military road from Number Four to Crown Point. These New England men made very extensive explorations of the valley of Lake Champlain as well as of the Connecticut and the intervening streams, and when the peace came, there were many of those soldiers ready to occupy the fair land they had seen.

The first of these was Capt. Samuel Robinson, of Hardwick, Massachusetts. He had been the captain of a company in one of the Massachusetts regiments in the campaigns of Lake George in 1755 and 1756; and in going through the wilderness, on his return from one of these campaigns, he accidentally came to what was afterwards Bennington, where he encamped for the night. He was so much pleased with the appearance of the country that he determined to make settlement there. Accordingly he took an early opportunity to ascertain who were the owners of the land he had seen, and finding that the land had been granted by Governor Wentworth of New Hampshire to some people in Portsmouth, he went to Portsmouth, got title to that township, and in 1761 he with his neighbors and friends, some of whose names are found in the muster rolls of his company in the war, started the first permanent settlement in Vermont west of the Green Mountains.

# CHAPTER II.

## NEW HAMPSHIRE CHARTERS.

As the title Captain Robinson got was a very material feature of the contests that afterwards ensued, it seems proper to notice somewhat in detail the authority given to Governor Wentworth to give charters to the township of Bennington and to other townships in the disputed territory.

For some forty or fifty years the provinces of Massachusetts and New Hampshire had been united under one colonial governor, although their governments were otherwise distinct. In the year 1737 there had come to be a dispute between the councils of those provinces in regard to the boundary between them. The province of Massachusetts, or Massachusetts Bay as it was then termed, had been created by a special charter from the crown of England, in which its northern boundary was described as a line drawn three miles north of the Merrimack river at the most northerly part of that river, and thence extending west to the Pacific Ocean. At the time this charter was granted, the Merrimack river had been explored only a few miles from its mouth, and, so far as it had been explored, its general course was from the west towards the east, making a bow or bend to the north and thence turning southeast to its mouth in the Atlantic.

Further exploration of the country, however, showed that the Merrimack river, for the most of its course, was a stream flowing from the north toward the south ; and the Massachusetts council, by a literal construction of the language of that charter, claimed jurisdiction and ownership of all the land west of that river to a point three miles north of its source. This source was the junction of two rivers, in what is now the town of Franklin, New Hampshire. A line extended west from that point would cross the Connecticut river in the vicinity of what is now Windsor and would include that part of the present state of Vermont south of Windsor and of Rutland. Under this claim, what is now Concord, the capital of the State of New Hampshire, was settled by Massachusetts people, and twenty-eight townships were granted by Massachusetts under their claim of ownership. On the other hand, the New Hampshire council insisted that the true meaning of the charter was, that the line extending west should start from the most northerly portion of that part of the Merrimack river which had a general easterly course, and that the discovery that the actual course of the Merrimack was different from that understood at the time of the charter, should not be held to give to the province of Massachusetts land that was not contemplated when its charter was granted. This dispute was referred to the privy council in England.

The privy council was an institution of which we have no counterpart in this country. In theory its functions were simply to advise the king in respect to his official actions, and its determinations took the form of "orders of the king in council." Originally the king was sovereign in fact as well as in name and his determinations embraced all departments of government, legislative and judicial as well as executive. As the development of the english constitution progressed and the different departments of government came to exercise the functions which have now been accorded to them, the functions of the privy council became more and more limited, but in the early part of the eighteenth century and until the discussions arose about the control of parliament over the colonies, the privy council had very largely the entire direction of colonial matters. This direction was both legislative and judicial in its character. In so far as the orders of the king in council made provision for what it was supposed the public good required, these orders were in the nature of legislative enactments and were wholly prospective in their operation. The privy council had also jurisdiction to determine certain appeals,—mostly those coming from the colonies. Some of these determinations were judicial in their character and had a retrospective effect; but its judicial functions were never very clearly defined.

Upon this dispute between the provinces of New Hampshire and Massachusetts, the privy council might have made a construction of the terms of the charter of Massachusetts which would have been a judicial decision of the dispute between the two provinces. What the council did do on that question was to set aside the boundary named in the charter, and to establish an entirely new boundary, giving the province of New Hampshire a strip of land about twelve miles wide,— more than it had ever claimed. The determination of the king in council was to enact that the boundary between Massachusetts and New Hampshire should be

a west line starting three miles north of the most
southerly portion of the Merrimack river, clearly ignoring the express language of the boundary of the
charter which started that west line from the most
northerly part of the river.  It was then claimed by
english lawyers that the king, by the advice of the
privy council, could, in his own discretion, revoke
any charter that had previously been granted either to
a colony or a corporation.  Since the decision of the
great Dartmouth College case some seventy years ago,
it has been the accepted law both in this country and
in England, that charters that have been acted upon,
cannot be revoked, even by the sovereign authority;
but at the time of the decision in question there was
little dispute about the full control of the king over the
boundaries of his colonies.

    This enactment of the king in council was a great
surprise to the Massachusetts authorities.  To say that
they were angry at the result, would be a very inade-
quate statement.  Believing that their Governor Belcher
had not fairly represented their interests, they made
a great clamor for his removal, and got in his place
Governor Shirley, an english lawyer whose practice
had not been large enough to prevent his acceptance of
a colonial office, and whose wealth, if any he had, was
not sufficient to place him above the temptations which
usually assailed the colonial governors of those times.
After he came, there was a good deal of wild talk
about ignoring the decision of the king in council, but
the only tangible result of that talk was, that Governor
Shirley undertook in 1744 to confirm a title claimed by
a dutchman named Lydius to a tract of about seven
hundred square miles of land extending along the Otter

Creek and for about sixty miles south of its mouth. As this tract of land was, for the greater part, entirely outside of what was ever claimed to be the boundary of Massachusetts, and as Governor Shirley had never any jurisdiction nor authority outside of the fixed boundary of the province, his confirmation of that title was of no avail.

After this decision of the privy council Benning Wentworth was appointed governor of the province of New Hampshire. His commission authorized him to exercise jurisdiction over the province of which one boundary was defined in the commission as follows:

"Bounded on the south side by a similar curved line pursuing the course of the Merrimack river at three miles distance on the northern side thereof, beginning at the Atlantic Ocean and ending at a point due north of a place called Pawtucket Falls, and by a straight line drawn from thence due west across the said river *until it meets with our other governments.*"

The commission also authorized Governor Wentworth, with the advice of his council and under moderate quit rent to be reserved, to dispose of such lands within the province as were under the disposition of the king:—

"Which said grants are to pass and be sealed by our seal of New Hampshire, and being entered on record by such officer or officers, as you shall appoint therein, *shall be good and effectual in law against us, our heirs and successors.*"

The order fixing the boundary of the provinces provided that the line designated should be surveyed by commissioners appointed by each of the provinces. Two surveyors were appointed by Governor Wentworth for New Hampshire, but the Massachusetts council in a

sulky manner refused to have anything to do
with the survey ; and so the line was run by the two
New Hampshire surveyors alone.

There was nothing in the commission to Governor
Wentworth, nor in any other of the orders of council,
that had then defined the western boundary of either
Massachusetts or New Hampshire. There was an
understanding that the province of New York extended
to a line twenty miles east of the Hudson river, so,
when the surveyors for New Hampshire ran out the
line between the two provinces, they extended it to a
point twenty miles distant from the Hudson river.
Eight years after the making of this survey, Governor
Wentworth made a charter of the township of Bennington, in which the boundaries were designated with
reference to a marked tree on the survey line between
the provinces, which tree was designated as twenty-four
miles east from Hudson river, and from that tree running six miles at right angles to the province line to a
certain hemlock tree, and thence the boundaries
of a township six miles square were designated, having
its southwest corner four miles west of the hemlock
tree. This statement of the controversy between
Massachusetts and New Hampshire has been made in
detail because it illustrates the effect of the orders of
the privy council upon the title of the lands affected.
Although Concord and those twenty-eight townships
that had been granted by Massachusetts had been transferred to New Hampshire, the title to all those lands
was confirmed in the grantees of the Massachusetts
colony.

Starting from the boundaries of this town of Bennington, Governor Wentworth, in the year of 1761 and

the following years, made grants of a large portion of the land now known as Vermont, on the west side of the mountains. On the east side of the mountains what is now the Town of Vernon had been included with some land on the other side of the Connecticut river in the charter of the Town of Hinsdale, granted by the province of Massachusetts before the change in the boundary. There was also a tract of land on the west side of the Connecticut river extending from Hinsdale up the river twelve miles, six and one-half miles in width, which had been conveyed to the province of Connecticut in exchange for some lands belonging to Connecticut that had been encroached upon by Massachusetts. These "equivalent" lands had been sold by Connecticut to a syndicate, of which Colonel Brattle and Lieutenant Governor Dummer of Massachusetts were leading members. North of that, there had been granted by Massachusetts, under the designation of Township Number One, a township now known as Westminster, as well as other townships in New Hampshire. After Governor Wentworth had assumed jurisdiction over these townships granted by Massachusetts, he made new grants to the claimants under the Massachusetts grants. That part of Hinsdale west of the Connecticut river afterwards became the township of Vernon. The equivalent lands were divided into three townships named Brattleboro, Dummerston and Putney, and Township Number One was regranted as the township of Westminster. After the close of the war, Governor Wentworth continued his grants until the number within the present state of Vermont became between one hundred and thirty and one hundred and forty. The number most frequently given is one hundred and thirty-eight.

His manner of procedure is illustrated by his grants on the Connecticut river. He had a survey made on the ice in the winter time and marked the trees on the bank of the river at intervals of six miles. These marks were made the corners of the townships. He then had three tiers of townships platted and from those plats he made the charters. In this way during the year 1761 every township except four on the Connecticut river was chartered, and before July 1764 more than one-half of the present state had been covered by these grants. The grantees of these charters were in a few instances men who intended to settle upon the lands they had so acquired, but were very largely land speculators, who took only to sell again. In looking over the names in the different charters it will be found that there were different syndicates, as we would now call them. Townships were granted to the Hunts and Hubbards and Willards, men prominent in the early settlements of Brattleboro and several New Hampshire towns. Their acquisitions covered several townships on Connecticut river, and some towns as far north as what is now Franklin county. Most of the grantees appear to have been men from Massachusetts and Connecticut, but one township, Essex, was conveyed to people from New Jersey, and two townships, Ferrisburg and Charlotte, were granted to Benjamin Ferris and his associates. Ferris appears to have been a Quaker, residing in what was termed the "Oblong" in Dutchess county, New York. Sometimes his residence is stated as the "Oblong" and sometimes as "Quaker Hill." Most of the townships in Chittenden county and some in Washington county were granted to Edward Burling and Thomas Willis and their associates, from whom were named the towns of Burlington and Williston. Nearly all of these men are said to have been residents of Westchester county, New York, although it appears that some of the grantees lived in New Milford, Connecticut; and friend Benjamin Ferris appears associated with the Westchester people in some of the townships. These. charters to Burling and Willis were dated June 7th and 8th, 1763, at which date the charter business of Governor Wentworth appears to have reached its flood tide.

These charters were of townships as nearly as practicable six miles square, each containing something over twenty-three thousand acres. They not only embraced conveyances or deeds of the land to the grantees, but also included grants of corporate franchises of townships. They had provisions for the allotment of the towns between the proprietors, the election of officers to conduct the municipal business; and they showed their anglo-saxon origin by providing for another institution which is especially dear to all yankees, the New England town meeting,— that nursery of incipient orators and budding statesmen. Each of these townships had about sixty proprietors, with his share of three hundred to three hundred and fifty acres. In each one of these townships a tract o five hundred acres was reserved for the governor. In some of the charters that was named as two shares; in some of the others this governor's right was described as an exception to the grant. There was also one right granted to the Society for the Propagation of the Gospel,—a London society,—one share for a globe for the church of England, one share for the first settled minister of the gospel and one share for the benefit of schools; and there was also a quit rent of one shilling for every one hundred acres after the first ten years, and a reservation of all pine timber fit for masts.

The principal purpose of making these grants by the colonial governors, was to secure to themselves the fees. The fees demanded by Governor Wentworth were not generally very large. Mr. Hildreth in his history states that they were one hundred dollars a township. In fact, however, there was no uniform price. It was usually supposed that fees fixed by law would be uniform, but there was no more uniformity in Governor Wentworth's prices than there is in the prices of a Chatham Street store. It appears from the history of Rutland that the fee paid for the charter of that town was one hundred dollars. The fees paid for the charter of Underhill were two hundred and thirty dollars and forty-one cents, and for Burnet the expense of procuring the charter was two hundred and nineteen pounds, or about seven hundred dollars.

There was not much difficulty in getting charters, provided the applicants would pay the fees. In fact, it seemed to be the principal business of all the colonial governors to make as much out of their offices as possible. Governor Wentworth is said to have got rich out of the fees he received, and his charges were mild in comparison with those of the New York governors. Governor Clark, in New York, from 1736 to 1743 is said to have cleared one hundred thousand pounds out of his office, and Governor (Admiral) Clinton is said to have made eighty-four thousand pounds in ten years. It was not alone the stamp tax and the tax on tea that was oppressive to the colonists. Their whole system of colonial government was managed to satisfy the rapacity of the government, and to further favoritism to those in power ; and as a result, that system was miserably inefficient for any good purpose.

These charters of Governor Wentworth had, many of them, as grantees the names of parties living at Portsmouth and supposed to be included in the inner circle of the governor's friends, or, to use the expressive but slang expression of these days, were within the "ring." We find the name of Richard Wybird very common in the list of grantees, and also Theodore Atkinson, who was secretary of the governor's council, and occasionally the names of Meshech Weare and John Wentworth. It is very probable that these men worked themselves in as proprietors of the townships as "dead heads." Governor Wentworth's reservations of five hundred acres to himself, so far as the charters granted within what is now the territory of New Hampshire were concerned, got him into trouble after the expiration of his term. The reservations were clearly illegal, because in making these charters or conveyances of land, he was acting simply as the agent of the king, and nothing is better settled in law than that an agent cannot donate to himself any property of his principal. There was not much contest in the Vermont grants upon this question. Eight of these reservations were granted by Governor Colden of New York to other parties, which was the most satisfactory grant made by any of the New York governors. Governor Wentworth did not, however, get much profit from these reservations as they were mostly lost through tax titles and in the disturbances growing out of the contest with the New York governors.

After getting the title to the lands in Bennington, Capt. Robinson commenced a settlement. Within four years, or by the summer of 1765, the settlement of Bennington embraced by actual count sixty-seven families, occupying as many separate farms. These settlers had cleared up lands and fitted them for-cultivation, had constructed houses, such as they were, and out-buildings, had made roads and established three schools in the town, built a meeting-house, had established a church with a settled minister, and had also built a saw mill and a grist mill. Of the neighboring towns, Arlington was probably next in the state of settlement and improvement. There must have been within that town forty or fifty heads of families. They had both saw and grist mills, built and owned by Remember Baker, whose name became prominent a few years later. These settlers were from Connecticut. Further north, on the Battenkill river, was the settlement of Manchester, less advanced ; but by 1765 it had become pretty well started towards the establishment of a town. Next north of that, the settlement of Dorset had just begun, and still further north, Danby was starting. These last three towns were settled mainly from the eastern part of Dutchess county, New York. Among these settlers were some quakers from near Nine Partners in Dutchess county, New York, which in those days appears to have been notable in Quaker history. Danby was afterwards spoken of by Ethan Allen as "Quaker Danbo." The only settlement north of Danby was at the falls of the

Otter Creek, where is now the City of Vergennes, and
where some settlers from Salisbury, Connecticut, had
improved the water power by the construction of a saw
mill and had taken up some lands in the town of
Panton. In the town of Shaftsbury, between the towns
of Bennington and Arlington, were quite a number of
settlers, and there were probably some in Sunderland
between Arlington and Manchester. There were also
some in Pownal. Just how many of those settlers there were, is pretty hard to determine, as no
records were kept and the only evidence we have is
from traditions collected by the town historians in the
Vermont Gazetteer. It is probable, however, that not
less than two hundred families had located in Bennington county on as many farms.

On the east side of the mountains there were more
settlers. Fort Dummer was built in 1724 and that
settlement had existed for more than forty years. In
Hinsdale there had been two forts built a few years
later, and the misfortunes of those settlers and their
captivity by indians were noted in our early school
books. It does not appear just how many settlers
there were in Hinsdale, now Vernon, but it is said that
in 1763 there were three frame dwelling-houses raised
in one day. Brattleboro was getting to be a place of
some importance, and ambitious of being made the seat
of the now county in contemplation. There had been
a fort constructed on the great meadows in Putney
some time previous to 1740, and settlements had been
made near that fort. There were settlements in Rockingham near what is now Bellows Falls and in the immediate vicinity of the fort on the other side of the river in
Walpole built by Colonel Bellows. Dummerston was

settled in 1752 by Capt. John Kathan; Chester was
settled in 1762; Halifax and Guilford, a little earlier.
Pretty soon after the close of the war, settlements had
been commenced in Springfield, Weathersfield, Windsor,
Hartland and Hartford. One settler had started in
Norwich, several in Thetford. There was quite an
extensive settlement at Newbury in connection with
another across the river at Haverhill, and there was a
settlement in the upper Coos at Guildhall. The settlement at Westminster was probably the largest in the
eastern part of the present state and had fifty families
in the summer of 1765. Rockingham had twenty-five
families in 1765.

Some years later it seemed to be in the interest of
New York officials to diminish the statement of the
number of actual settlements in the New Hampshire
grants, and so in 1771 there were put among the
colonial records some affidavits and official statements.
One affidavit stated that there were not over sixty families in the whole of the Connecticut river valley on the
west side of the river. The statement of Mr. Simon
Stevens, who was a prominent adherent of the New
York claims during the whole controversy, fixed the
number at seventy and claimed that some of those were
squatters, having no claim of title to the land they
occupied. Colonel Samuel Wells of Brattleboro, who
was the agent of the New York claimants in that
vicinity, stated that in his opinion there were not over
seventy settlers; and another statement was that there
were less than one hundred. None of these statements
are worthy of any credit. From the actual facts
appearing not only from accredited historians but the
colonial records of New York themselves, it is certain

that they were so wide of the truth that they could not
have been honestly made. On the twentieth of January, 1766, there was a return made to the colonial
office in New York, by name, of over six hundred men
between the ages of sixteen and sixty, subject to military
duty, who were residents in the south part of that territory east of the mountains and west of the Connecticut
river. This enumeration must have been made the
summer before, or in the summer of 1765. The same
return gives an estimate of the numbers for the north
part of the same territory at three hundred. A census
was taken of the inhabitants of that region in 1771, in
which it was shown that the number of heads of families
was something more than seventy per cent. of the
number of enrolled militia. There is no reason for
supposing that this proportion was materially different
in 1765. That would give over four hundred heads of
families or settlers in the summer of 1765 for what was
afterwards Cumberland county alone. The estimate
made in the return of Colonel Chandler for the north
part of the territory under consideration was undoubtedly too large, and, instead of being half as many as
in Cumberland county, one-fourth would have been
about the proportion as shown by the census. It is
pretty safe to say that in the summer of 1765 there
were more than five hundred settlers in the valley of the
Connecticut on the west side of the river. Each of these
settlers had started a farm, had cleared some land and
had built a cabin or a house to live in. The extent of
these improvements varied in proportion to the length
of time the settlers had been there. Capt. Kathan of
Dummerston had cleared one hundred and twenty acres
of land, had built a house and barn, a saw mill and

works for the manufacture of potash. This is the largest improvement of which we have any account. It is probable that many of the settlers had no more than five or ten acres of clearing and that most of their cabins were small. Still, it must have taken twenty days' work to clear an acre of that land, and it was no small task to build even a small log cabin. There was no little work in the construction of roads. It is pretty certain that wherever a farm had been taken up and improvements started, the value of the improvements was much larger than the original value of the land, and that for each of these farms the value of the improvements must have been from one hundred dollars upwards.

# CHAPTER III.

The settlement of the new state was brought to a sudden check and the grants of townships by Governor Wentworth were entirely stopped by the publication in April, 1765, of the proclamation of the lieutenant governor of New York, announcing the order of the king in council, making the Connecticut river the boundary between New York and New Hampshire. This order had been procured upon the application of Lieutenant Governor Colden of New York to the privy council. The lieutenant governor, and acting governor of the province of New York at that time, was Dr. Cadwallader Colden, who took a very prominent part in all the proceedings out of which grew the difficulties between Vermont and New York.

Born in Scotland in 1688, educated as a physician, Dr. Colden came to Philadelphia in 1716, to New York City two years later, was in 1720 made surveyor general of the province, and two years later a member of the governor's council, which position he retained until the time of his death in 1776. He was the most prominent and active member of the provincial government and by far the ablest man connected with its administration. He was beyond question a man of ability, a scientific

writer and an historian of no small capacity, and thoroughly conversant with the situation and history of the province.   He was far superior to the regular governors of
New York.   Indeed, the colonial governors of New
York with one exception, Gen. Monckton, were not
men of ability nor integrity.   They were usually the
needy retainers of some of the court favorites, appointed to office by reason of the influence of their
backers, whose chief official ambition was to make the
most of their official opportunities for their personal
benefit.

For many years Dr. Colden was senior member
and president of the provincial council, and it is said
that he was the chief adviser of Governor Clinton.
Between him and Lieutenant Governor De Lancey there
was a rivalry.   The province of New York was controlled by several large families who owned most of
the lands under settlement.   Although Colden had no
family connections and but little property when he
began, he was enabled by his great ability to hold his
own against his rivals.   He seems to have been at
times in alliance with the Livingston and Clinton families, but not on intimate terms with the Schuylers.   In
a little volume of the colonial history of New York,
written by one of the Schuyler family, Dr. Colden's
career is depicted in not over friendly terms.   He was
accused by his rivals of taking advantage of his official
position as surveyor general to get hold of large
quantities of public lands; but he was able to deny
these charges and challenge his accusers to their proof.
If not actually innocent, he was adroit enough to con-
ceal his holdings.   In respect to the Vermont lands it
is certain that he did not get for himself any very

large quantity, as did some of the other governors. It appears that when the claims of the New York grantees were adjusted, his estate held about nine thousand acres. That was no more than he could have naturally acquired from the soldiers' grants that were so freely offered in the market, without any suspicion of taking advantage of any official position. Indeed, so far as the Vermont lands were concerned, the fees he received for the patents he issued as governor were more valuable than any profits he could have made from the lands themselves. He was a zealous advocate of the tory claims of the right of the english government to tax the colonies and had written memorials on that subject that had attracted the favorable attention of the extreme english tories.

When Lieutenant Governor De Lancey died in 1761, Dr. Colden succeeded to the government as president of the council. He was then seventy-three years of age, but vigorous and daring as a young man. When the New York assembly undertook to pass a law by which the judges of the courts should become independent of the crown, he very promptly vetoed the act and so left the judges dependent for their offices upon the arbitrary caprice of the government. When, after the death of De Lancey, who was chief justice as well as lieutenant governor, it was questioned whether any good New York lawyer would accept the position of chief justice, he very promptly disposed of the question by importing a chief justice from another province. By this devotion to the prerogative of the government as against the colonists, he became a favorite of the Earl of Halifax, then secretary for the colonies, and was by that influence appointed lieutenant governor. He was four times afterwards called to be the acting governor of the province.

When Governor Wentworth made the first charter in the new territory, that of Bennington, in 1749, he wrote a courteous letter to Governor Clinton of New York, informing him that he was directed by the king to make grants of unimproved lands, that applications were made for some townships in the western portion of those lands, and, wishing to avoid interfering with the government of New York, he inclosed a copy of his own commission and desired to be informed "how far north of Albany and how many miles east of Hudson river to the northward of Massachusetts line his (Governor Clinton's) government by his Majesty's commission extended." To this Clinton replied, very likely by the advice of Colden, "that this province is bounded eastward by Connecticut river, the letters patent from King Charles II to the Duke of York, expressly granting all the lands from the west side of the Connecticut river to the east side of Delaware Bay."

The learned author of the history of Cumberland county seems to regard this inquiry of Governor Wentworth as an admission that Wentworth was doubtful of his authority to make any grants beyond the Connecticut river. Mr. Davis is a good lawyer and his opinion of the construction of a writing deserves the highest respect. It would seem, however, that Governor Wentworth's inquiry indicates no more than an expression of doubt as to the exact location of the line between the colonies. This claim on the part of New York was very different from the description of the boundaries of New York made by Governor Colden, while he was surveyor general in 1738, in which he

states that the west line of Massachusetts is the eastern
boundary line of New York. This is shown by his report
quoted at length by Governor Hull in the latter's Early
History of Vermont. It is proper to acknowledge here
that many of the facts mentioned in this paper are taken
from Governor Hull's book, and that the whole book
contains a very thorough and fair representation of all
the facts shown by the official record.

Some correspondence ensued between the two governors, and it was agreed to refer the matter to the decision of the king in council, but no action was taken
upon this reference, and nothing was done about the
boundary until 1763.

On June 25th, of that year, at the request of Governor Monckton, then about to embark for Great Britain, a committee of five members of the privy council
of New York, among whom were Judge Horsmunden,
Oliver De Lancey, and Lord Sterling, made an official
representation on the subject of the boundaries of the
province. In respect to the boundary with New Hampshire their report had this language:

"The jurisdiction as well as the property of the
soil yet unappropriated in both governments appertains
to his Majesty. It depends on the Crown by its own
authority to fix and assertain (sic) the limits between
them.

We are humbly of opinion that it will not be inconvenient to either province if his Majesty should be
pleased to Order that the same line which shall be established as the Devision between them and the province of Massachusetts Bay be continued on the same
course as far as the most northerly extent of either
province, with a saving to the inhabitants of New York
of such lands as are held by grants under the great seal

of that province eastward of Hudson's river beyond the distance of twenty miles, etc."

Upon Governor Monckton's departure for England Lieutenant Governor Colden again succeeded to the government. On the 26th of September he forwarded to the board of trade a memorial, claiming that the five gentlemen of the provincial council were mistaken in regard to their statements, particularly in reference to the Massachusetts boundary which was then unsettled. In regard to New Hampshire, he stated that that province was bounded on the west by other governments, and there was no pretense of its extending west of the Connecticut river, which was the eastern boundary of New York, and he averred that there was no reason why the boundary of either Massachusetts or New Hampshire should be established at the twenty-mile line. The boundary of Massachusetts was established at the twenty-mile line ten years later, by the action of commissioners appointed by both provinces. Governor Colden's paper contains this further language :

"If all the lands in the province of New York from twenty miles of Hudson's river to Connecticut river were given up, the Crown would be deprived of a quit rent amounting yearly to a large sum, in my opinion, greater than the amount of all the quit rents that would remain and is now received.

The New England governments are formed on Republican principles, and these principles are zealously inculcated on their youth in opposition to the principles of the constitution of Great Britain. The government of New York on the contrary is established as nearly as may be after the model of the English constitution. Can it, therefore, be good policy to diminish the extent of jurisdiction of his Majesty's province of New York to extend the power and influence of the others?

The commerce of the inhabitants on the east side of the Hudson river to a great extent eastward, probably as far as Connecticut river, is with the towns on Hudson's river. It must then be extremely inconvenient to them to be under different laws, different jurisdictions and different currencies of money."

It will be seen that this communication was addressed to the legislative discretion of the privy council, because its claims were based on what was alleged to be the public good in the determination of the disputed boundary. It has been stated that Governor Colden also sent petitions purporting to be signed by large numbers of the residents of the territory in question, in which they ask to be attached to New York for the reason that it was more convenient for them to have business relations with that province than with New Hampshire. Many writers have accepted this statement as true, among whom is Mr. Palfrey, the author of the History of New England, although he questions the good faith of such petitions. On the other hand Governor Hall, after patient examination, finds no evidence of any such petition. Governor Hall is undoubtedly correct, for it is due to Governor Colden to say that his character, while not free from censure, was above the use of any such unworthy means, and subsequent events establish the fact that no such petitions could have been made in good faith.

The communication of Governor Colden produced the result he desired. A letter was written to him by the lords of trade July 13, 1764, in which they say:

"As the reasons you assign for making Connecti-

cut river the boundary line between the two provinces
appear to us to have great weight, we have adopted and
recommended that proposition."

On the 20th day of July, 1764, an order in council was made, referring to this report of the board of
trade and using this language :

"His Majesty taking the same into consideration
was pleased with the advice of his Privy Council to approve of what is therein proposed, and doth accordingly
hereby Order and declare the western banks of the river
Connecticut, from where it enters the province of Massachusetts Bay as far north as the 45th degree of north
latitude to be the boundary line between the said two
provinces of New Hampshire and New York."

It has been, and is still claimed, that this expression
"to be the boundary" was ambiguous, because it was
uncertain whether this order was a decision that the
western bank of the river named had previously been
the boundary between the provinces, or was an enactment that afterwards it should be such boundary. This
is the claim of Mr. B. H. Hall in his History of Eastern
Vermont, and also that of the author of the History of
Cumberland County already referred to. If the whole
record is considered, there can be no ambiguity. From
that it appears that the action of the privy council was
not a judicial trial. There was no hearing of any appeal.
Both in form and in substance the proceeding was
wholly of a legislative character. In form it shows a
reference to a committee, a report and the adoption of
that report. In substance it was a declaration that the
public good would be promoted by the establishment of
the boundary named. Such was the opinion of some
of the members of the privy council who made the order. Lord Hillsboro, who was a member of that coun-

cil and afterwards secretary for the colonies, wrote to
Governor Moore :

"I think fit to send you a copy of his Majesty's
order in council of the 24th of July, 1767, forbidding
any grants to be made of the lands annexed to New
York by his Majesty's determination between that colony and New Hampshire."

Again in December, 1771, he wrote to Governor
Tryon :

"I have long lamented the disorders which have
prevailed on the lands heretofore considered as a part of
New Hampshire, but which were annexed to New York
by his Majesty's order in council on the 20th of July,
1764."

And again in 1772 he writes about the country
which had been annexed to New York. Lord Dartmouth was secretary for the colonies after Lord Hillsboro, and his letters to Governor Tryon speak of the
royal instructions respecting the district annexed to
New York.

These citations show clearly that the order fixing
the boundary was not in fact, nor was it regarded by
the men who made it, a decision or determination that
the boundary had been as it was then established, but,
on the contrary, a legislative order by which certain
lands, formerly supposed to belong to New Hampshire,
had been annexed to New York.

This distinction is important on the question of
title to the lands. If the order of 1764 had been a decision that the province of New Hampshire had never
extended beyond Connecticut river, there would then
be ground for the claim that no title could come from
charters given by the New Hampshire officials. There
is no doubt, however, that this order of the king in

NEW YORK LAND SPECULATORS.

council was precisely like what we have seen was the order by which a portion of Massachusetts was annexed to New Hampshire,—a legislative provision entirely prospective in its operation which had no effect upon the rights of parties claiming title to the land embraced in the order.

When the proclamation of Governor Colden announcing the decision of the boundary line was first promulgated, it was not supposed that the change of boundary would interfere with the title of the settlers to the lands they had purchased and improved. That proclamation appears to have been a surprise to all the settlers. There had indeed been a proclamation in December, 1763, announcing the claim of New York to the Connecticut river as a boundary, but this does not appear to have come to the notice of any of the settlers. It is to be remembered that in the new settlements at that time there were no telegraph lines and in fact no mails. There were very few newspapers in the whole country and fewer still came to those settlements.

When, however, during the summer of 1765, they found surveyors, claiming to act under New York authority, about to run lines upon their lands, the settlers began to think there was trouble with their titles. Upon further inquiry they found their worst fears were only too well founded. Governor Colden had commenced making sales of their homes and before the first of November following, he had sold over one hundred thousand acres of these lands, nearly if not quite all of which had been included in the charters given by Governor Wentworth. He had sold, on the 21st of May, 1765, a tract of land called Princetown, nominally to a company of twenty-six persons, but

within a few days this company conveyed the whole
tract to three persons, John Taber Kempe, James
Duane and Walter Rutherford. These men were New
York land speculators. Kempe was attorney general,
and Duane a leading lawyer. This tract covered most
of the settlements of the town of Arlington, all of those
in Manchester and all of those on the Battenkill river
between Arlington and Manchester, and also ground on
which there were probably some settlements in the
town of Sunderland. This tract covered the ground
on which there were probably fifty farms, more or less
improved, and also included the new grist mill and
saw mill which Remember Baker was then building at
the place where is now the village of East Arlington.
Nine days later, on the 30th day of May, there were
sold some of the improved lands in Bennington to a
man named Slaughter, upon which purchase Slaughter
brought one of the ejectment suits that cut such an important figure a few years later. Sometime during the
same season about ten thousand acres of land in Bennington and Pownal were sold to one Crean Brush.
Brush was then a New York lawyer and land speculator,
had been employed in the office of the provincial
secretary, had got into the government " ring " and
was afterwards sent to Westminster, Vermont, to look
after the interest of the New York grantees as well as
his own extensive interests in the grants. He was the
first lawyer who ever settled in Vermont, but nobody
will now claim that he was ever a credit to the profession. Governor Colden also sold lands in Shaftsbury
to a man named Small, and on the strength of that title
the latter brought an ejectment suit against Josiah, or
rather Isaiah, Carpenter, which was the suit actually

tried at Albany some years later. In fact, Governor Colden had before the 1st of November sold and issued patents for all or nearly all of the lands in Bennington county that had been occupied by the settlers.

The governor's operations were brought to a sudden check by the enactment of the famous stamp law, which took effect on the 1st day of November. By that law no charters or deeds of land, or warrants for survey of land, were valid unless stamped with the government stamp. There was a very general uprising in the colonies against the stamp act, and the stamps were seized from the officers having them in charge; and Governor Colden was forced to give up those sent to the colony of New York, so that he could not comply with the law and stamp his patents. This state of things continued until the following summer, when the repeal of the stamp act permitted further issues. In the meantime Sir Henry Moore had been made governor.

# CHAPTER IV.

When the settlers found they were in danger of
losing their farms, they got together and appointed
Capt. Robinson of Bennington, and Jeremiah French of
Manchester a committee to go to New York and see
what could be done about perfecting their titles.
When they arrived in New York they found Sir Henry
Moore in office, but could get no satisfactory reply to
their application for confirmation of their titles. In
fact, there were two reasons why they could not then
get confirmation. Most of their lands had been sold to
speculators and just at that time the lack of stamps
prevented the issue of confirmatory patents. There
was talk about the amount of fees that were to be
demanded by the New York governor. Capt. Robinson's statement is, that he found their title could not be
confirmed without payment at the rate of twenty-five
pounds New York money for every one thousand acres
of land. That amounted to about fifteen hundred dollars a township. They found also that for these fees
they could only get land of inferior quality, the best
land having been sold to the speculators.

There were other efforts made at the same time to
procure confirmation of these New Hampshire titles. It

appears from the proprietors' records of the little town
of Maidstone in Essex county that there was a proprietors' meeting at Stratford, Connecticut, in the fall of
1766, at which an agent was appointed to go to New
York and attend a meeting of the agents and proprietors
of the New Hampshire grants, to be held on the 10th
of the following December for the purpose of seeing
what could be done to protect their titles.  A further
record shows that, the conference in New York having
failed, the proprietors voted to send an agent to attend
another meeting of delegates of the proprietors of
different towns to be held at the house of Friend Benjamin Ferris in "The Oblong," and that at that meeting
it was decided to send an agent to England to apply to
the king for relief.  In the meantime the settlers of
Bennington and of the adjoining towns had come to a
similar conclusion; and the result was, that it was
agreed that Capt. Robinson should go to England for
the benefit of the settlers and grantees.

It was also determined to secure the services of
William Samuel Johnson, Esq., agent of the province
of Connecticut, to assist Capt. Robinson in his application.  Capt. Robinson was fortunate in finding in
control of the British cabinet the Earl of Chatham and
the special friends of the American colonies.  In the
privy council, to whom his petition was presented,
were Lord Chancellor Camden, Lord Shelburne and
Secretary Conway, who were, next to Lord Chatham,
the most steadfast advocates of the colonies.  The
Archbishop of Canterbury was also very favorably
inclined to his petition, not only on general principles,
of justice, but from his special interest in the church
and the Society for the Propagation of the Gospel.

Capt. Robinson made his petition to the privy council with the assistance of Mr. Johnson. It was signed by himself in his own behalf and in behalf of more than one thousand other grantees. This petition was delivered to Lord Shelburne, secretary of state for the colonies, on the 20th of March, and a petition was also presented by the Society for the Propagation of the Gospel, to which had been granted in the New Hampshire charters one right out of each township. That society was interested in the matter because in all the New York grants nothing was reserved either for that society or for the church of England. Very soon after the receipt of that petition Lord Shelburne wrote to the Governor of New York a letter in which he gave this direction :—

"I am to signify to you his Majesty's commands that you make no new grants of those lands, and that you do not molest any person in the quiet possession of his grant who can produce good and valid deeds for such grant under the seal of the province of New Hampshire until you receive further orders respecting them.    *    *    *

In my letter of the 11th of December I was very explicit on the point of *former grants*. You are therein directed 'to take care' that the inhabitants lying westward of the line reported by the Board of Trade as the boundary of the two provinces, be not molested, on account of territorial differences, or disputed jurisdiction, for whatever province the settlers are found to belong to, it should make no difference in their property, provided that their titles to their lands should be found good in other respects, or that they have long been in the uninterrupted possession of them. His Majesty's intentions are so clearly expressed to you in the above paragraph, that I cannot doubt of your having immediately, upon receipt of it, removed any cause of those complaints which the petitions set forth, if not, it is the King's express command that it may be done without the smallest delay. The power of granting lands was vested in the Governors of the colonies originally, for the purpose of accommodating, not distressing settlers, especially the poor and industrious.''

The letter also proceeds to comment on the unreasonableness of obliging the settlers to pay a second time the immense sum demanded in fees. With this letter were forwarded copies of the petitions of Capt. Robinson and the Society for the Propagation of the Gospel. To this communication and the petitions Governor Moore made extended replies on the 9th and 10th of June. On those days he wrote four letters to Lord Shelburne, of which three were upon this subject. The first one, covering over fifteen closely printed octavo pages in the documentary history of New York, was devoted to the petition of Capt. Robinson. It was a rambling, discursive letter, disingenuous and evasive. In the first part of his letter he referred to the minutes of the provincial council, by which it appears that the order of the king in council establishing the boundary on the Connecticut river was communicated to the provincial council on the 10th of April, 1765, and then he recited the order of council of the 22nd of May of the same year, requiring the surveyor general not to return surveys of any lands actually occupied by settlers. This was literally true, but the manner of its statement was such as to create a false impression. Its purpose was, undoubtedly, to carry the idea that the provincial council by making this order had intended to secure the rights of actual settlers. It would naturally be presumed from the date so ostentatiously shown,—the

first notice of the order establishing the boundary being
in April and the order prohibiting the surveyor general
to return surveys of land occupied by settlers being in
May,—that the order would cut off all encroachments
on lands occupied by settlers. Governor Moore omitted to state, however, that on the very day before this
order was made a patent had been issued for the grant
of Princetown, covering 26,000 acres of the best land
in the province, and that the record showed a survey
commencing "one hundred forty chains westward of
John Holley's House," which included that house within
the limits of the lands granted. It was true that the
order recited had been disobeyed in respect to every
grant of lands in Bennington county that were occupied by settlers, and that all or very nearly all the
improved lands in that county had been granted in
disobedience to that order.

Governor Moore further made parade of what he
called an order of the provincial council, that from
the lands granted to one Small there should be reserved
two hundred acres for each of the settlers actually
upon the land. If any such order was passed, it was
entirely ineffectual, because it was the case of this same
Small against Carpenter, actually tried at Albany, in
which judgment was rendered against Carpenter, although he was in actual possession of his farm before
Small's grant.

Governor Moore also devoted nearly a page of his
letter to a statement that Capt. Robinson and a Mr.
Cole had applied to him and his council for relief, that
he was himself their advocate before the council recommending that they be allowed to retain their farms,
that the council did so determine, and that the council

further declared that they should have their lands without any fees, for which he states that Cole and Robinson were very grateful, and took occasion to follow him into his private parlor to express that gratitude. There was no occasion for any gratitude. If there had been any such order of the council it was worthless, because, on careful inspection, it appears from the governor's own statement that their lands had already been granted away. In fact, judgment in ejectment was afterwards rendered against some of these same parties.

Governor Moore further claimed that a large part of the land occupied by these settlers was situated within less than twenty miles of Hudson river. This was untrue in fact, but, as it was then the common claim among the New York speculators, it cannot be charged that in this respect Governor Moore was guilty of intentional falsehood. In another part of the same reply, however, the governor cannot be so excused. He devoted several pages of that reply to a statement of the great things he had done and was about to do for the benefit of settlers on the New Hampshire grants. He stated that he had determined to engage personally in a plan for the settlement of a township twelve miles north of the north boundary of Cumberland county, which was to be distributed to poor families on small farms; that as soon as those terms were made known, applications were made by different persons for grants and no less than fourteen families were already settled on it; that he had proposals from ten more then living in New York; that as the giving of lands alone to those people was not sufficient without other assistance, he had at their request ordered a saw mill and

grist mill to be built for their use; and that as there
was no building in that part of the country yet appropriated for divine worship, he had directed a church to
be built at his sole expense, in the center of the township, and should set apart a large farm as the glebe for
the incumbrance.

All this, if it had been true, would have been no
answer to the claims of Capt. Robinson and his associates. There was, however, not a word of truth in
the whole statement. The township described as situated on Connecticut river twelve miles north of the
boundary of Cumberland county was the township of
Bradford. There had been application for a charter o
that township under the name of Mooretown made by
one John French and his associates, and, before the
arrival of Governor Moore, Governor Colden had the
papers prepared for the issue of the charter. When
Governor Moore assumed control of the government,
he refused to permit the charter to be issued without
the payment of full fees which were over ninety dollars
for every one thousand acres. After Governor Moore's
death the charter was issued to William Smith, author
of the History of New York, and twenty-four associates;
and that charter recites that the original petitioner,
French, had deceased, and that Smith and his associates
represented the same parties.

The history of Bradford was written up for Miss
Heminway's Gazetteer in 1868, and was well written by
the Rev. Mr. McKean. In that history the charter
issued to historian Smith is set forth in full and a full
account of the early settlement of the town is given.
There were not fourteen families settled in that town at
the time of Governor Moore's statement, and not one of

the settlers who were then there had come on account
of any inducements offered by Governor Moore. Governor Moore never built or procured the building of
any mills nor of any church, nor did he ever expend a
penny for the benefit of settlers.

Governor Moore's letter in respect to patent fees
was evasive. He said that he never made a demand
for fees either from Mr. Robinson, or from any other
person, but had always thought himself happy in
having an opportunity (sic) in remitting them to those
he apprehended would be distressed in paying them.
He never did remit any part of the fees for confirmation of any New Hampshire charters. It might be
literally true that he did not make demand of Mr.
Robinson, because, as the most of the Bennington
lands had already been granted to New York speculators, it was out of his power to make confirmation
upon any terms. It might have been true that he had
not in person demanded any sum from any other
person. His agents, however, had made demand for
the full fees. Mr. Isaac Miller was agent of the heirs
of Governor Dummer and the other proprietors of
Dummerston. In a letter he wrote to one of his
principals he states the fact, that Colonel Samuel Wells
of Brattleboro as agent for the New York Governor
had demanded fourteen hundred and forty dollars for
the confirmation of the patent of that township. That
township covered one-third of the forty-eight thousand
acre tract known as the "equivalent" lands.

Governor Moore in his answer undertook to
weaken the claims of the New Hampshire grantees by
affirming that their expenses in obtaining their charters
were less than they pretended. As we have seen,

Governor Wentworth's fees were by no means uniform, but there is no evidence that any charter was granted by him upon the terms named by Governor Moore.

The conclusion of this remarkable document contained an expression of indignation at the presumption of a man who, having followed "one of the lowest and meanest occupations, at once sets himself up for a statesman, and from a notion that the wheels of government are as easily managed as those of a wagon, takes upon himself to direct the king's ministers in their department."

He had previously stated that Capt. Robinson's service in the then late war had been nothing more than driving an ox cart for sutlers. This was not true. Capt. Robinson's name appears upon the muster rolls of Massachusetts as the captain of a company of militia which was in actual service during two campaigns and engaged in the battle in which Colonel Williams lost his life. Even if that statement had been true, it would have been a very insufficient answer to the claims of the men who had purchased their land in good faith from the officers of the government, who had for many years been in actual possession and control as agents of the owner, and who, relying upon that purchase, had made large expenditures of labor and means in the improvement of their homes. That statement is more discredit to the governor than to Capt. Robinson.

The answer to the petition of the Society for the Propagation of the Gospel claims that in some of the townships for which he had granted confirmatory charters the rights of that society were protected. He admitted that in one township this confirmation was omitted and he neglected to state that in all of the grants on the west side of the mountains that society had been wholly ignored. He claimed that he had prepared to grant a whole township to the church of England, which he claimed would be more than an equivalent for the one share the society had lost. The records show no evidence of any such township, and the whole history of the time shows this statement of Governor Moore to be utterly false.

The reply to these communications of Governor Moore came more promptly than was usual in the proceedings of the privy council. On the 24th day of July, 1767, an order of the king in council was passed, repeating the prohibition to the governors of New York from making any grants of lands described in Mr. Robinson's petition and in the petition of the Society for the Propagation of the Gospel until the further pleasure of the king. It is said, and so Mr. Robinson reported at home, that at the time that order was passed a majority of the privy council were in favor of making a further order confirming the titles under the New Hampshire grants; but the president of the council, Lord Northington, objected that such an order had better be made on a regular appeal and that the council was also very much occupied with other matters. This president of the council was the ex-chancellor of whom it is related by Lord Campbell, in the "Lives of the Lord Chancellors," that he applied to the king to be relieved from holding evening sessions of his court because he wanted to get drunk after dinner. Whatever may have been the immediate reasons, Lord Northington was entirely right. An order confirming a title could be made only in the exercise of the judicial functions of the council. That required a regular ap-

pearance of all the parties interested and a full hearing
on the merits of the claim.

Had the Chatham ministry remained in power, it is
very probable further relief would have been granted
to the settlers, and perhaps they would have been restored to the jurisdiction of New Hampshire, because, as
we have seen, that ministry was the most favorably inclined to do justice to colonies ; but the reaction of the
high tory element against the tidal wave that had caused
the repeal of the stamp act had already commenced.
Lord Shelburne was very soon afterwards driven out of
the secretaryship, and a new ministry, of which Charles
Townsend was the leading spirit, was formed.   The
prime object of that new ministry was to establish the
right of taxing the colonists, and out of that contest
grew the American Revolution.   There was no disposition on the part of the new officers to approve the oppressive measures of the New York government, and so,
we find letters of Lord Hillsboro and Lord Dartmouth
condemning those acts in language identical with that
of Lord Shelburne ; but in their disapproval the new
administration was handicapped by the pressure of the
great contest then coming on.   In their contest with
the colonies it was necessary for the administration to
cultivate all the loyalty it could among the colonists.
In New York the royalists were almost all included in
the circle around the royal governors, and it was not
considered wise to alienate the few friends they had in
the colony.   So the proceedings of the New York governors were passed by with censure, where, under other
circumstances, they would have met more decisive treatment.

during the Walpole administrations and in the first part of the eighteenth century, miserably corrupt and inefficient, its judicial administration had come to deserve high rank. It had already furnished Lord Hardwick and Lord Camden for chancellor and was about to give Lord Mansfield for chief justice; and there was not a country where private rights were more carefully protected than in England.

Governor Moore died early in September, 1769, and upon his death Lieutenant Governor Colden again succeeded to the administration.

## CHAPTER V.

### EJECTMENT SUITS.

Soon after the death of Governor Moore, the holders of the New York titles commenced active measures
to assert their claims. Their first attempt was upon
the land of Mr. James Breakenridge, who lived in the
northwestern part of the town of Bennington. He had
a farm of considerable extent which, without being no-
tified of any adverse claim, he had occupied and improved for many years. There had been made by the
New York government, in 1739, a grant of a tract of
land called "Walloomsac," which was claimed to extend over a part of what was included in the township
of Bennington. According to a plat or map made on
paper, it embraced some two or three thousand acres in
Bennington, including the whole of Mr. Breakenridge's
farm. According to Ethan Allen's account of it, in
1774, the limits of that patent, as shown by the lines
actually surveyed, included only about thirty or forty
acres in Bennington. If the monument described by
Allen was not upon the line of the actual survey, then
there was no actual survey of the eastern boundary of
that patent.

On the 19th of October, 1769, commissioners were
sent from Albany to make surveys on Mr. Breakenridge's farm under some quit rent statutes of New York.
This proceeding was evidently preliminary to an action

of ejectment. By some means Mr. Breakenridge had notice of the approach of these commissioners, and on the day of their arrival, October 19th, they found present not only Mr. Breakenridge himself, but most of his neighbors, including the minister, the Rev. Jedediah Dewey. Some of these men had guns with them, but they were all engaged in the peaceable avocation of harvesting corn. Without using any actual violence, or, so far as appears, making any boisterous threats, they induced the commissioners to withdraw without doing the work for which they had come. The New York authorities claimed that it was a riot and thereupon indictments for riot were found against Mr. Breakenridge, Mr. Dewey, Mr. Robinson and others. This was the first actual resistance to the claims of the New York speculators. Without doubt, their actions technically constituted a riot, although the parties implicated could truthfully assert the old formula, that they used no more force and violence than was necessary to accomplish their purpose,—that of preventing the operations of the commissioners. It was the first deliberate resistance to the royal authority in the colonies. There had been, prior to that, it is true, some effervescent uprisings against the stamp act, but this was the first instance in which the people of any of these communities, including their most conservative men and the minister of the parish, united in a deliberate yet stern resistance to what they deemed the oppression of the rulers set over them. It was, undoubtedly, an act that had been carefully considered and had been made the subject of prayer as well as of consultation. It was a brave act, because the settlers were few in number and not rich, and they were defying the authority of a powerful colony.

Here in this little opening in the forest and in the mellow sunlight of that autumnal day was begun a contest out of which grew the establishment of a new state and the development of those traits of character still peculiar to the people of that state. It was in some respects the initial contest of the American Revolution, although the settlers had then no intention of opposing the English Government because they had reason to believe that, when they could reach that government, they could find redress for their wrongs. This contest was, without doubt, the genesis of a new state.

The men engaged in this contest and the clergyman who led them were none of them land jobbers nor speculators. There was no display nor flourish in their resistance, and they were not afraid to encounter the great odds against them. This resistance was not any manufactured excitement wrought up by reckless men. Ethan Allen had no part in it. He was then unknown to fame. Seth Warner was undoubtedly there, because he was a neighbor of Mr. Breakenridge, but his presence attracted no attention. Remember Baker was then building his second mill at Pawlet. Ira Allen was either a school-boy of eighteen years in Salisbury, or, possibly, a young surveyor running lines in the woods of Hubbardton. These men of Bennington started the new state alone and unaided.

At the same time the New York claimants either began ejectment suits or pushed forward those ejectment suits that had previously been begun. There was one suit against Mr. Breakenridge, another against Mr. Fuller of Bennington, another against Mr. Carpenter of Shaftsbury, and another against Mr. Rose of Manchester; and it was understood that suits had either been commenced or were likely to be commenced against all of the settlers in that vicinity, and that there were claimants for all of the improved lands in what is now Bennington county.

The prosecution of these suits required united action for their defense, and here was the first public appearance in the grants of a man whose name and fame are co-extensive with the state of Vermont and about whose name is woven much of the romance attached to its early history. He has been called the Robin Hood of Vermont. It would seem more appropriate to designate him as a William Tell. Yet his character and history were unique, and no other designation so well fits him as that of the Ethan Allen of Vermont.

Allen was at that time thirty-two years of age. He was a native of Litchfield county, Connecticut, the son of Joseph Allen and his wife, Mary Baker. He was the oldest of eight children, of whom six were boys. His youngest brother, Ira, was, next to Ethan, the most prominent figure in the early history of the state. His father was a farmer living in limited, if not straitened, circumstances in Litchfield and the neighboring town of Cornwall, where he died when Ethan was about seventeen years of age. The family moved to the neighboring town of Salisbury, where it seems that Ethan had spent some time as a student and where under the instruction of the village minister he had been nearly fitted for college; but the death of his father prevented further advance in his studies. He worked for some years on the farm in care of his father's family, and, some time after their removal to Salisbury, he got some interest in an iron furnace in the northern part of the township near the Massachusetts line. Of his history at that time very little is known. He was married in 1762, and shortly after his marriage took up his home just across the line in Sheffield, Massachusetts, but, it would seem, continued his business in the iron furnace until about the time he went to Vermont. Although his legal home was in Sheffield, Massachusetts, he was usually counted as an inhabitant of Salisbury, Connecticut. That little town of Salisbury appears to have been the parent of more of the Vermont settlers than any other town. From it came the settlers of many of the towns in Bennington, Rutland, Addison and Chittenden counties, and from the same town came also the first settler in St. Albans in Franklin county. It is a little town nestling among the hills that form the water shed between the Housatonic and Hudson rivers. It had, about the year 1740, become prominent by reason of iron mines discovered within its boundaries; and for years the iron manufactured in that vicinity was largely used in the colonies and had great reputation for a superior quality. It is situated in the northwestern corner of the state of Connecticut, joining, on the north, the town of Sheffield in Massachusetts, and, on the west, that extension of Dutchess County which we have seen was designated "The Oblong." The town probably never had more than two or three thousand inhabitants; but four men, each one of whom had more to do than any others with the early history of the state of Vermont, had lived within its borders. These men were Ethan Allen, Thomas Chittenden, Ira Allen and Nathaniel Chipman.

Just when Ethan Allen first came to Vermont is a matter about which statements are conflicting. Prof.

Zadock Thompson, who devoted much time to a study of the life of Ethan Allen, fixes the date of his coming to Vermont as 1766. Governor Hall, whose researches, if not as extensive, are quite as reliable, fixes it at 1769. The editor of the collections of the Vermont Historical Society and of the Proceedings of the Governor and Council of the early state, adopts Prof. Thompson's statements, while most other writers, including the late Henry Hall, author of an unfinished work on the "Life of Ethan Allen," fix the date at 1769. In the town history of Hubbardton, found in the Gazetteer, there is mention of a rumor that Ethan Allen was interested in the original proprietorship of that township, and there were stories that some of the marked trees bore the initials of Zimri and Ira Allen. That historian does not, however, mention any titles or records of titles derived from Ethan Allen, and there is no evidence found of his having had any such title. If any of the Allens had anything to do with Hubbardton, it must have been in 1709 or earlier; because, after that date, their presence is well accounted for elsewhere. It would seem very probable that in 1709 the two younger Allens might have been employed as surveyors of that township. They were educated as land surveyors and their circumstances rendered it necessary that they should seek employment as soon as they could. The first president of the Vermont Historical Society advances the theory that Ethan Allen was interested in some of the patents issued by Governor Wentworth. There is, however, no evidence to warrant the statement that he had any interest in the Vermont lands until five years after the last patent from New Hampshire, and he must have

continued in his furnace business for some time in
order to have obtained the means to get the interest in
the lands he afterwards held.

What interest he first got or how he acquired it is
entirely a matter of conjecture. It is known that Benjamin Forris and others got charters to the townships of
Charlotte and Ferrisburg, and that Edward Burling and
Samuel Willis and their associates, got lands in Colchester, Williston, and Burlington in Chittenden county.
It is known that, at some time between 1769 and 1777,
Ethan Allen, with three of his brothers and Remember Baker, who was a cousin of the Allens, got title to
most of the lands in those four townships. The names
of Benjamin Ferris and of Edward Burling appear, with
others, among the names subscribed to the powers of
attorney given to Capt. Robinson when he left for England. Allen's name does not appear among those names,
although the list includes several who must have been
his near neighbors. In Prof. Thompson's "Life of
Ethan Allen" it is related that he early became acquainted with Dr. Thos. Young, who resided in "The
Oblong," and from him derived some peculiar religious
notions, or, rather, notions in regard to religious sub-
jects. It is very likely that he was also acquainted with
Benjamin Ferris, who resided in the same vicinity. We
have seen that there was a meeting of the proprietors
of the grants at the house of Ferris at "The Oblong,"
at which it was determined to send an agent to England
upon failure of getting satisfaction from Governor
Moore. It seems probable, therefore, that the good
Quaker, being by religion as well as by nature averse
to contests, is likely to have been very willing to dispose of his interest in the grants and perhaps to have

given credit for some, if not all, of the purchase money. This would just suit Allen, who could not have had much money, but who was not of a timid disposition, and by no means a peaceable Quaker. Judge Chipman, in his "Life of Nathaniel Chipman," tells us about the Allen family and their lack of means. Ethan Allen must have acquired a little something out of his furnace operations which had extended over a period of eight or ten years. Heman and Levi Allen had been partners in a country store in Salisbury, and Prof. Thompson gives a copy of the notice of dissolution of that partnership, which appears to have occurred February 3, 1772. We find that shortly afterward, Levi Allen was the purchaser of the New Hampshire titles to the towns of Georgia and Swanton in Franklin county. Levi Allen was not a member of the Onion River Company, although it is so stated in Judge Chipman's book. The proprietors records of Colchester, written by Ira Allen himself, give the names of the members of that company. It was composed of Ethan Allen and his three brothers, Heman, Zimri and Ira, and Remember Baker. At a later period the members of this Onion River Company became the owners of the largest part of eleven townships of the New Hampshire grants and Ira Allen acquired large interest in the lands sold by the state of Vermont.

The Allens were, undoubtedly, land speculators in the fullest extent of that term. They cannot claim, as could the settlers at Bennington, that they were innocent purchasers of those New Hampshire grants. They took their titles, such as they got, with full notice of the adverse claims, and most likely the existence of those adverse claims made the former holders of the titles they got willing to dispose of them at prices within their reach.

This character of land speculators adhered to them in their intercourse with their fellow-settlers, and was, probably, the chief cause of the lurking distrust with which they were regarded by the other settlers of the new state. It may be a matter of surprise to those whose ideas of the Allens were formed from reading the novels of which they were the heroes, to learn that they were personally unpopular among the settlers; yet such was the fact. Although they both had a wonderfully magnetic power over the men with whom they came in immediate contact, yet, outside of those under the influence of that immediate contact, they were regarded with distrust. When the Continental Congress had authorized the formation of a battalion of Green Mountain Boys and had given authority to select their own officers, a convention of the committees of the several towns was held at "the inn of Cephas Kent in Dorset," in June, 1775. At that convention the officers of the new battalion were selected by ballot, and Seth Warner was elected lieutenant colonel over Ethan Allen by a vote of forty-one to five.

Although Ira Allen had been the most active member of the new state government, he never could get any higher place than that of member of the council and state treasurer. He twice failed of an election by the people, and the second time he was also defeated by the legislature. He never afterwards attempted to get any state office. On account of his connection with the Allens Governor Chittenden was himself defeated in the election of 1789. A thorough investigation of all the matters of complaint vindicated the governor, and he was afterwards continued in office until the last year of his life. Ira Allen's accounts as state treasurer were examined by a commission, of which his successful rival was a member; and, though they embraced details amounting to hundreds of thousands of pounds, he showed vouchers for every penny of his disbursements. For a man of his opportunities and training, the accounts he presented were wonderfully accurate.

For this jealousy with which the settlers regarded both the Allens, when in fact they were not deserving of censure but had, both of them, deserved well of their neighbors and of the new state, no explanation can be given except the fact that they were land speculators.

Before the Revolutionary War Ethan Allen spent most of his time in Vermont, although his family remained at Sheffield until 1777. In some of the proclamations offering a reward for his arrest, he is described as resident in Bennington, but it does not appear that he ever had any permanent home in that town. Previous to 1769 or 1770, he had, undoubtedly, by purchase of some of the rights of the original grantees, become interested in the New Hampshire grants. These rights so purchased probably included several obtained from the Ferrises and Burlings.

When the trial of the ejectment suits was about to come on at Albany, he was interested in the result; and therefore took very active part in preparing the defense to those suits. He went to Connecticut and employed Mr. Jared Ingersol, a prominent attorney in that province. There was not at that time a lawyer within what is now called the State of Vermont. He also went to Portsmouth, New Hampshire, and procured official copies of the commission to Governor Wentworth and the other papers necessary to show the title under which the settlers claimed.

A trial of some of the ejectment cases was had at Albany. The bill of exceptions in one of the cases has been preserved and it shows a trial before Judge Robert R. Livingston and Judge George Duncan Ludwig on the 28th of June, 1770, of an action of ejectment in favor of John Small against Josiah Carpenter for lands in the town of Shaftsbury. The plaintiff claimed title under a soldier's grant made by Gov. Colden dated October 30, 1765. The defendant offered in evidence the charter of the town of Shaftsbury authenticated by the seal of the province of New Hampshire, dated August 20, 1761, showing title in himself. The court rejected that evidence, assuming to take judicial notice that at the date of the charter the land in question was not in the province of New Hampshire but was in New York. All the evidence of defendant's title being ruled out by the court there was, as a matter of course, nothing left to go to the jury, and the verdict was necessarily for the plaintiff.

# CHAPTER VI.

The correctness of this ruling and the merits of the claims to the land of these grants are matters about which people have disputed for more than one hundred years and it is very likely this dispute will continue until the whole thing is forgotten. The land in dispute was an improved farm, in possession of which the defendant had been for several years prior to the commencement of plaintiff's title. At the time of this trial there was no statute like the present statutes of Vermont and many other states for the relief of parties who had taken land under an apparently good title and who, relying upon that title, had made permanent improvements. By the harsh rules of the common law, then in full force, there was an absolute forfeiture of all improvements in case of a recovery in ejectment by the plaintiff.

The grant under which the plaintiff claimed was made in direct disregard of the orders of the provincial council, made May 22, 1765, prohibiting the surveyor general from including in a return of surveys made by him any land in actual occupation of a settler. The loss of these improvements was unquestionably a great hardship to the settler. The order of the provincial council cited, as we have seen, so prominently by Governor Moore in his reply to Lord Shelburne was never intended to be obeyed and was made only for the purpose of conveying a false impression. The whole history of grants in that county shows a deliberate purpose on the part of speculators to select improved lands for the sake of getting the benefit of those improvements.

The claim of title to these lands rests upon a purely technical question of law. The most prominent feature of these claims has been overlooked by nearly every one who has taken part in the discussion about them. Both the provinces of New York and New Hampshire were royal provinces, in which the title to the lands belonged, not to the colonies or provinces, but to the crown of England. All the charters or conveyances were in the name of the king of England and were executed by parties claiming to be the authorized agents of the king. The title to those lands was precisely like the title now held by the United States government to lands in our western states; and the material and decisive question was, simply, who was authorized by the king to make those conveyances. There was nothing in the official character of the governor of either province which of itself gave him that authority. The authority of the governors of both provinces to grant lands was contained in special instructions partaking of the nature of powers of attorney. These were subject to revocation and, after they were revoked, neither the governor nor the provincial council had any more authority to make grants of land than would the ordinary agent after the revocation of his power of attorney. None of the advocates of the New York claims have ever recognized this fact, and it was entirely overlooked by Judge Livingston in his ruling in the case of Small against Carpenter. It was, however, recognized by Judge Chipman in a case growing out of the charter of Windsor (Jacob v. Smead 1 D. Chip. 50); and was also recognized by Mr. E. J. Phelps in his oration at Bennington in 1691.

Another important consideration in this discussion is found in the fact that, while the New York claims made large account of the grant of Charles II to the Duke of York, their claim of title was not under the grant to the Duke of York, but adverse to it. If there had been any claim of title coming from that grant, it would have accrued to the heirs of James II, and not to the crown of England. The title would have come to the Chevalier St. George and his son Charles Edward, instead of to George III. The original grant to the Duke of York, afterwards James II, was a proprietary grant, like that of Pennsylvania to William Penn or of Maryland to Lord Baltimore. The New York claim was, that when the Duke of York became king, his proprietary title merged in the title he held as king of England. That was the opinion of James himself and his advisers, as we find by his instructions to Governor Dongan in the year following his accession to the throne. It is probable, however, that, instead of a merger, this was a surrender of his proprietary title. However this may be, whether by merger or by surrender, the fact remains that his proprietary title became extinguished. There is no doubt about the law of merger. When one title is merged in another it becomes absolutely extinguished, just as effectually as a chalk mark is wiped out on a black-board, and the result is precisely the same as if no such title had ever been granted. Ethan Allen, although not a lawyer, was a man of vigorous intellect and in his argument, made in 1774, although

he did not profess to understand anything about the
law of merger, he pointed out the absurdity of the New
York claim being both adverse to, and dependent upon,
this grant to the Duke of York. The extinguishment
of this grant left the condition of the title the same as if
it had never been made.   All there was left, then, was
the name of New York applied to the province, and all
that could be claimed was what would be presumed from
the establishment of a province by the name of New
York.  If in other respects it appeared that the boundaries of the province of New York were the same as of
the land grant to the Duke of York under that name,
then there would be a presumption that this boundary
by the Connecticut River was intended by the King as
the boundary of the province of New York.  This
argument, however, is entirely overthrown by the fact
that not one foot of the boundaries named in the grant
to the Duke of York was ever accepted as a part of the
boundary between the province of New York and the
adjoining provinces.  The grant to the Duke of York
was, in terms, a grant of all the land lying between the
Connecticut River and Delaware Bay.  Undoubtedly at
the time of making that grant, the officers of the crown
had only in mind a strip of land bordering on the sea
coast of a uniform width, extending inland as far as the
bay itself.  In fact, however, the Connecticut River flows
about four hundred miles.  A straight line drawn from
its source to the head of Delaware Bay would cross the
state of Vermont somewhere near the town of Bennington.  It would not include the land in the town of
Shaftsbury claimed in this ejectment suit, and would
not include the present City of Albany, but would take
in what is now the City of Philadelphia.  Not even the

most zealous advocate of New York can now claim that the west line of the grant was ever recognized as the west line of the province of New York. Again, the line of the Connecticut River was expressly disavowed as the eastern boundary in the case of Connecticut and Massachusetts. The boundary of Connecticut had been established as early as 1650, while New York was a Dutch Province, and the boundary of New York and Massachusetts was settled in 1773.

After the merger or surrender of the title of the Duke of York, the land came back to the king as original proprietor, and he had perfect control over it and the right to make in his discretion any disposition in respect to it. He had also the right arbitrarily to revoke or change any previous order or disposition. On the sixth day of September, 1744, an order was made by the king and council reciting that Fort Dummer had come within the province of New Hampshire and directing the authorities of that province to make provision for its maintenance. It is true that New Hampshire neglected to obey this order, but the question here is, not what New Hampshire did, but what the owner of the land directed with regard to the boundaries of his provinces. If there had ever been anything equivalent to an order that the Connecticut River should be the eastern boundary of the New York province, this order of the king and council made in 1744, had the effect of repealing such prior order; and from that time until the order of 1764, the Connecticut River was not the boundary between New York and New Hampshire. The order of 1744 did not of itself designate any boundary in place of the prior one so repealed by it. If then, there ever had been an order designating the Connecticut River as the eastern boundary of the New York province, the most that could be claimed was, that after the repeal of that designation, the boundary was left indefinite.

Here, then, belonging to one owner, was a large tract of territory consisting of two parcels which were defined only by the fact that one was east of the other, and that one was called New York and the other New Hampshire. The eastern part of this tract had been put under the control of one of the owner's agents, the governor of New Hampshire; the western part had been put under the control of another of the same owner's agents, the governor of New York. But, even if no authoritative definite designation by the owner of the dividing line between these two parcels was then in force, nevertheless, such a line could at any time be designated by the king himself in any manner he saw fit. In 1755 a map was published, and it had upon it the certificate of the accredited agents and officers of the king in respect to his colonial lands. That certificate is quoted by Governor Hall on page 50, of his Early History, and reads as follows:

"This map was undertaken with the approbation and at the request of the lord's commissioners for trade and plantations, and is chiefly composed from draughts, charts and actual surveys of different parts of his Majesty's colonies and plantations in America, a great part of which had been lately taken by their lordship's orders and transmitted to this office by the governors of said colonies and others.

Plantation Office, February 13, 1755.

JOHN POWNAL, Secretary."

There were other maps of the same kind. Mr. L. E. Chittenden, in his late volume mentions a map, still

in existence, which is dated in 1762, and dedicated to
Charles Townsend, and which shows the boundary between New Hampshire and New York the same as the
map above referred to.

The effect of published maps as instruments of evidence in questions of titles to land has been a matter of
frequent examination by the courts of this country, and
the principles upon which they may be received in evidence are now pretty well settled. Those questions
most frequently arise upon claims of dedication of
streets and public grounds in new cities, and they
present the exact question here under consideration,
viz., what is proper evidence of the intention of the
owner of land in respect to the use and disposition of
that land. It was held nearly one hundred years ago
in a case involving the public use of the streets and
public grounds of the city of Cincinnati, that, where
a proprietor made a map of lands he owned, and that
map showed that on certain parts of his land there was
a public street or park, the making of that map was
evidence of the intention of the owner of the land to
dedicate that street to the public use. Following that
principle, it has more recently been held that, where a
map made by other parties was brought to the attention
of the owner of the land and he used it in his dealings
with parties in respect to that land, he, by that act
ratified the map and made it his own for such purpose. On the same principle, when the king of England by his accredited agents approved this map of 1755
and authorized the makers of it to publish it to the
world with his certificate, it was a clear indication of his
intention that the land embraced in his two provinces
of New York and New Hampshire should be divided

according to the line shown on that map. The division between New Hampshire and Massachusetts on that map was a substantial prolongation of the western lines of the provinces of Connecticut and New York, and that, in the absence of any express designation to the contrary, would be sufficient evidence to establish the New Hampshire title. The decisions referred to, while they have been made since the trial of the action in Judge Livingston's court at Albany, are simply declaratory of general principles of law which existed at that time and which should have controlled the action of that court.

Again, even if the boundary between the two provinces had been left wholly undefined by the king, the terms of the commission to Governor Wentworth authorized him to extend the jurisdiction on the line west "until it meets our other governments." That gave Governor Wentworth authority to take possession of the unoccupied lands between the two provinces. Upon that authority in the spring of 1741 he sent his surveyor, Mr. Richard Hazen, to run the line between his province and that of Massachusetts. This Mr. Hazen did, and marked it on the ground to a point within twenty miles of the Hudson river. That was the first actual occupation of the lands beyond the settlements near Fort Dummer until the lands described in the Hoosic and Walloomsac grants were reached. According to the utmost claim for the extent of those grants, they did not include the farm of Mr. Carpenter, which was the subject of that suit at Albany. In November, 1749, Governor Wentworth sent another surveyor, Matthew Clesson, to survey the township of Bennington. That surveyor, commencing on the line previously surveyed by Mr. Hazen, and, taking one of the monuments marked on the ground in that prior survey for his starting point, surveyed and marked on the ground the boundaries of the township of Bennington. Twelve years later, Governor Wentworth sent another surveyor to run the lines of the township of Shaftsbury, whose survey commenced on the line previously surveyed by Mr. Classen for the boundaries of the town of Bennington, and who marked out on the ground the boundaries of Shaftsbury. Here, then, was a series of acts of occupation continuing for more than twenty years, in which the authorized agent of the owner of the land exercised upon that land visible acts of agency, purporting to be done under his authority as such agent. From that lapse of time and the absence of any interference on the part of the owner of the land, a ratification of his acts must be implied. It is true that these acts of possession were not such as would amount to a disseizin of the true owner, but they were sufficient to constitute an exercise of authority claimed under a power of attorney where there was no active exercise of authority under any other claim. To illustrate: if, instead of the king of England, George Washington had been the owner of the provinces of New Hampshire and New York and he had executed a power of attorney to John Adams, in which he states, "I hereby authorize John Adams to sell my lands in the eastern part of the two provinces," and he had given a similar power of attorney to John Jay, in which he says, "I hereby authorise John Jay to sell my lands in the western part of my provinces," and, acting under that power of attorney John Adams had sent out his surveyors and run and marked the lines just as Governor Wentworth did on these New Hampshire grants, and the other agent, John Jay, had paid no attention to them; there is no doubt that the deeds of John Adams would have given good title to any lands that had not been occupied under deeds from the other agent, and that until they struck the actual occupancy of other parties the title so made was valid. In the light of these principles of law, as they are now well settled, we can safely assert that the title of the New Hampshire settlers was not only an equitable but a legal title.

This conclusion is supported by a great weight of authority, both in England and America.

Among the numerous expressions of that opinion the following may be noted:

1. The official letter of Lord Shelburne, colonial secretary, in April, 1767, to the effect that the change of jurisdiction should make no difference in the property of settlers under former grants. Although the colonial secretaries were not always themselves lawyers, they had the benefit of advice of the law offices of the crown.

2. The unofficial opinion of the privy council, in 1767, at the time the official order was made prohibiting further grants by the New York governors.

3. The official opinion of Lord Dartmouth, secretary for the colonies, in reply to the letter of Governor Tryon citing the decision of the court in the Albany case in which he says:

"I do not conceive the titles of the present claimants or possessors ought to have been determined upon any argument or reason drawn from a consideration of what were or were not the ancient limits of the colony of New York. Had the soil and jurisdiction within the province of New York been vested in proprietaries as in Maryland, Pennsylvania, Massachusetts Bay, or other charter governments, it would have been a different question ; but when both the soil and jurisdiction are in the crown to limit that jurisdiction and to dispose of the property in the soil in such manner as shall be thought most fit, and after what had passed, and the restrictions which had been given respecting the claims, as well on Lake Champlain, as in the district to the west of Connecticut river, by which the King had reserved to himself the consideration of those claims, I must still have the misfortune to think, that no steps ought to have been taken to the prejudice of the claimants under the original titles."

4. The official report of the board of trade made to the privy council, Dec. 3d, 1772, and the approval of the recommendations of that report by the privy council made in the April following. The privy council always included among its members some of the best jurists and lawyers in the kingdom.

5. The decision of the English commissioners upon the application of John Monroe for reimbursement for his losses by reason of his adherence to the crown during the Revolutionary War. His lands, both in Vermont and New York, had been confiscated during the war. Under the provisions made by the English government, he was entitled to compensation for his losses. Upon consideration of his case, the commissioners decided to give him compensation for the lands he held in New York but refused to allow him anything for the lands he claimed in Vermont, because, they held, his title was not good, the land having been included in the grants made by Governor Wentworth. This appears from a letter from Monroe to Duane written at the close of the war. It would seem that these commissioners were the same as the commissioners of the board of trade having charge of colonial matters.

6. The decision of the supreme court of Vermont in the case of Jacob v. Smead already referred to. This decision may be fairly offset against the decision of the New York court and the character and standing of Chief Justice Nathaniel Chipman is, to say the least, equal to that of the New York judges. There can be no claim of local interest in favor of the New York court against the Vermont court.

7. There is, further, the fact that from the New Hampshire charter have been derived the unquestioned titles to most of the lands in the state of Vermont. It is true that in 1791 the legislature of the state of New York released its claims for a consideration paid in money. That release could not have affected the title of private individuals holding New York grants, unless it should be held that their acceptance of a dividend on the $30,000 paid by Vermont should be regarded as an estoppel against their subsequent claims. That the Vermont titles were held by virtue of the original New Hampshire charters, and not by virtue of any conveyance from New York, was established by two decisions of the supreme court of the United States,—those in favor of the Society for the Propagation of the Gospel against the towns of New Haven and Pawlet, in which its title as grantee under the New Hampshire charters was sustained against the townships which had become grantees under an attempt of the state to give those public lands to the townships. It is true that the validity of the New Hampshire charters was not the subject of the contest in those decisions, and both parties to the contest admitted their validity. If, however, the New Hampshire grants had been wholly void by reason of the lack of jurisdiction of the governor of

New Hampshire over that territory, the supreme court
of the United States should have taken judicial notice
of that fact and could not have rendered judgment in
favor of the Society.

Although the presiding judge in that Albany trial
bore a name that has since, in the person of his son,
become illustrious in American jurisprudence, his opinion of the law is not entitled to the credit of an
absolutely impartial judge. Governor Hall comments
upon the fact that Judge Livingston was the grantee
of a tract of 35,000 acres under the name of Camden,
and for that reason the inference is that he was interested in sustaining the New York titles. The facts,
however, acquit the judge of any charge of impropriety
on account of that interest. He received that patent
the November preceding that trial, but the lands described in that patent had never been granted by the
governor of New Hampshire; and there was no question of the conflict between the grants of the two
provinces. Judge Livingston's patent did not give
him a good title, because his patent was given after the
revocation by the king of the authority of the governor of New York to make conveyance of lands in the
New Hampshire grants. Upon the final determination,
these lands came to the state of Vermont and were
granted in its sovereign capacity. No such question
was presented in the trial at Albany and on that
account there was no impropriety in Judge Livingston's
hearing the case before him. There was another
ground, however, upon which the propriety of Judge
Livingston's action cannot be so well sustained. His
brother-in-law, James Duane, was very largely interested in lands granted by the governors of New York

and the final decision of the case on trial would determine Mr. Duane's rights. Upon principles now well settled, Judge Livingston ought not to have sat in judgment in a suit in which his brother was so largely interested. At that time, however, these principles of judicial propriety were not as well settled as they are now. In the very next year Lord Dunmore as the governor of the province of New York and *ex officio* chancellor of the province, undertook to sit in judgment in an action in the name of the king against Governor Colden, in which he himself was the plaintiff in interest, and had the hardihood to require a full trial and argument before himself; but before he came to the rendition of the judgment somebody told him more than he knew before about the authority of judges to decide cases wherein they were personally interested.

The evidence offered by the defendants on the trial of those ejectment cases was a deed from the sovereign who was the common source of title of both claimants; which deed was prior in point of time to the title claimed by the plaintiff. The evidence of the plaintiffs had already shown that the defendants were in possession. The court excluded that evidence on the ground that it could take judicial notice that the land in question was then the province of New York and that the boundary of that province had, previous to 1764, been so clearly defined and established by competent authority as to exclude the governor of New Hampshire from acting as the agent of the king in selling that piece of land. It is true that the extent of the boundaries of the state or province within which a trial is had is ordinarily a question to be decided by the court as a matter of law, upon facts of public history of which the court is said to take judicial notice. The only fact upon which this ruling is claimed to be based is the fact of the grant by Charles II, in 1664, to the Duke of York with the designation of the western bank of the Connecticut River as its eastern boundary. The mistake of the court in that trial was, in its ruling upon the effect of the grant to the Duke of York. That grant did not purport to convey the land in dispute to the plaintiff's grantors. To avoid the effect of that conveyance to the Duke of York and his heirs, it was claimed, and that claim is elaborately stated in all the published statements of the ground of that claim, that the Duke's individual title was merged in the title of the sovereign when he became King James II. When the title under that grant became merged in the original title of the sovereign, the grant was extinguished and not perpetuated. The land in question came to the crown in 1686 entirely freed from all the effects of the grant to the Duke in 1664 and of the re-grant ten years later. When that grant was extinguished by merger the effect was, that the land came back to the crown precisely as if no grant had ever been made. As we have already seen, the establishment of a province under the same name, New York, did not imply that the lands included in the province were the identical lands that had previously been named in the grant. The grant to the Duke of York covered all the land between the Connecticut River and Delaware Bay. That included most of the present state of New Jersey, part of Pennsylvania, but did not include more than a small part of the present state of New York. By strict construction the grant to the Duke of York would not include the cities of Albany or Schenectady, and by no construction could it be held to include the present city of Utica or any of the western part of the state. As we have already seen, the order of the king in council made in 1764 was wholly prospective in its operation. It was not a judicial decision, but a legislative enactment. It could have no effect to avoid vested rights that had been legally acquired before its enactment. In deciding the question under consideration,—namely, the validity of the charter of Governor Wentworth, made in 1761, —the facts are to be considered the same as if the order of 1704 had never been made.

Upon this subject even some writers of Vermont history have been misled into accepting as correct the extreme claims of the New York partisans.  Mr. B. H. Hall at the beginning of chapter 6 of his History of Eastern Vermont, uses this language:

"While New Netherland was a Dutch province, its northern limit had been placed at the river St. Lawrence and the fresh (Connecticut) river had washed its eastern borders.  When Charles II gave the province of New York to his brother James, its area included all the land from the west side of the Connecticut river to the east side of Delaware bay.  The governments of Massachusetts and Connecticut had in several instances encroached upon the territory claimed by New York, but the differences resulting from these trespasses had usually been amicably settled or at least temporarily adjusted.  Never until now had there been any attempt to deprive New York by systematic action of rights and dominion which she claimed as her own."

And again, on page 130 :

"By trespasses Massachusetts and Connecticut had extended their limits far beyond the line assigned them by the charter, but they had acknowledged the encroachment and by treaties New York had ceded to them the land on which they had attempted to usurp authority."

This language of Mr. Hall is, most likely, taken from the statement of the claim of New York reported by Crean Brush to the New York Assembly in 1773, which was said to have been drawn up by Mr. Duane and which was afterwards published and extensively circulated as a statement of the grounds on which the New York claims were based. It will be very difficult to find an instance where any reputable historian has accepted a partisan statement with more childlike confidence than Mr. Hall has accepted this statement of the New York claims, and it would be equally difficult to find an instance in which that confidence was less deserved.

While it is true that the Dutch did formerly claim to the Connecticut river, that claim was resisted by the province of Connecticut, and the Dutch were forced to yield, and did yield their claim; and the boundary between Dutch New York and Connecticut was settled by the treaty at Hartford in 1650, by which the boundary was established as a line ten miles east of the Hudson river. That line was accepted by the Dutch when they retook New York in 1673.

During the same year in which the grant to the Duke of York was made, 1664, the boundary between New York and Connecticut was established by commissioners sent by the king, of whom Governor Nichols of New York was one, and the boundary between the two provinces was fixed as, in general terms, a line tweny miles from the Hudson river. This award recites that the commissioners had heard the parties and they do

"Order and declare that the creek or river called
⁹Mamaroneck, which is reputed to be about thirteen miles
to the east of Westchester and a line drawn from the
east point or side where the fresh water falls into the
salt, at high water mark, north, northwest to the line of
Massachusetts be the western bounds of the said colony
of Connecticut. All plantations lying westward of
that creek and line so drawn to be under his royal
highness' government, and all plantations lying eastward of that creek and line to be under the government
of Connecticut."

It was claimed there was a mistake in the language
of that line, and another adjustment was attempted in
1683. This was recited in a report of the English
board of trade to King William, dated March 3,
1700, which report designated the line that now exists
between New York and Connecticut, and the line so
recommended by the board of trade was authoritatively
established by order of the king on the 4th day of
March, 1700. This line was resurveyed in 1731.
Upon examination of the maps of New York and Connecticut it will be seen that there is, in the south-
western corner, a part of Connecticut that extends
further towards the Hudson river than the rest of the
state and within less than twenty miles of the river.
To offset this, or as "equivalent" lands, Connecticut
yielded a strip about two miles wide in the western
part of Litchfield county; and it will be seen by the
map that on the eastern part of Dutchess county is a
narrow strip that extends as far north as the north line
of Connecticut to the east of Columbia county. This
little strip of land constitutes what is termed "The
Oblong" and was given to New York as equivalent
for the land taken by Connecticut within less than

twenty miles of the Hudson river.  The twenty mile
line was, in substance, established as the boundary to
which the provinces were entitled; and the only acknowledgment by Connecticut that it extended beyond
its boundary relates to that oblong strip for which this
equivalent was given.

In respect to Massachusetts, the quotation is
equally unfortunate.  Massachusetts never acknowledged any title of New York to the lands now occupied
by that state.  There was a controversy between the
two provinces for many years.  That was finally
settled by reference to arbitrators or referees agreed
upon by the provinces.  On the 18th of May, 1773,
the governors of the two provinces made an agreement
accepting the line fixed upon by these referees, by
which it was declared that,

"A line beginning at a place fixed upon by the
two governments of New York and Connecticut on or
about A. D. 1731 for the northwestern corner of a tract
of land commonly called the oblong, or equivalent
land, and running from said corner north twenty-one
degrees, ten minutes and thirty seconds east to the
north line of the Massachusetts Bay, shall at all times
hereafter be the line of jurisdiction between the province of Massachusetts Bay and the said province of
New York."

This was substantially a line twenty miles from the
Hudson river.  Instead of acknowledging any encroachment, both the colonies of Massachusetts and Connecticut always insisted upon, and after the close of the
Revolutionary War secured, large cessions of land on
their charter claims.  In 1786 the state of Connecticut received from the general government the cession
of lands in the Western Reserve, in what is now the

state of Ohio, amounting to about four millions of acres. In 1784 the state of Massachusetts brought, in what was then termed the federal court, its proper action against the state of New York, in which it claimed large quantities of land under its charter grants from the crown. To this claim an answer was made by Mr. Duane in behalf of the state of New York, and his brief is printed at length in the third volume of the collections of the New York Historical Society. The brief, however, was not very satisfactory because the New York authorities, without permitting the case to come to trial, settled the matter by conceding to Massachusetts between five and six million of acres of land in western New York, a territory as large as the whole of the present state of Massachusetts and at that time the most valuable land in the country.

Some writers of Vermont history have carried the impression that the action of the New York authorities was not very oppressive. Judge Daniel Chipman, who about fifty years ago wrote the life of his brother, Nathaniel Chipman, asserts that confirmation of the New Hampshire grants could have been procured at the rate of 70 pounds New York money a township; and Mr. Davis, who wrote the history of Cumberland county, published in the last volume of the series commenced by Miss Hemmenway, states that the action of the New York government did not seem to be "very oppressive."

The action of the New York government with regard to confirmatory titles was by no means uniform. The settlers of Bennington county could not have procured a valid confirmation of their charters at any price, because the colonial officers had sold land within every

one of those townships, before the settlers received notices of any claim against their titles.    Not only had
they sold lands within each township, but they had sold
almost every acre on which improvements were made
by the settlers.    When Captain Robinson and Mr.
French went to New York in 1765 they were not informed of all the facts that have since been shown to
have been true.    The petition prepared by Captain
Robinson before he left for England stated that they
found confirmation could not be procured without their
paying the fees of office at the rate of 25 pounds New
York money for every 1,000 acres of land.    This was
about nine times the sum named by Judge Chipman.
    The first confirmatory charter that was granted
was that of the town of Chester, made by Governor
Moore in July 1766.   Governor Moore issued confirmatory patents for six townships.    It appears from the
letter of Governor Colden to the colonial secretary,
dated January 4th, 1770, that Governor Moore refused
to pass any patents unless his full fees were paid; that,
before the arrival of Governor Moore he, Colden, had
prepared patents for the confirmation of several townships and had agreed with the proprietors on a reduction of the regular fees; but that he was prevented from
putting the seal to any of them by the arrival of Governor Moore, who afterwards took his full fees for one
of the grants which had been nearly ready for the seal
before he came.   This must have been the township of
Chester.    It appears that Colonel Thomas Chandler,
as the representative of the proprietors of Chester, then
called New Flamstead, went to New York in October,
1765, and made application for confirmation of his charter.   The new charter which he got bears date the July

following. At the convention held at Westminster in
July 1777 Colonel Chandler was present as a member;
and the record shows that he was also a member of the
committee appointed to make a publication of the reasons for the establishment of a new state. The report
of that committee was made to the adjourned session of
that convention held at Windsor in June following.
That report contained a statement of grievances, framed
upon the model of the Declaration of Independence.
Beside other complaints, was the statement that the
New York authorities had refused to give confirmations
of the New Hampshire charters except upon the payment of $2,300 for a single township. That statement
was copied by Ira Allen in the preamble to the constitution of the new state written by him the next fall.
This was undoubtedly the sum demanded of Colonel
Chandler for the confirmation of this township of Chester. As that township was larger than the average,
containing over 31,000 acres, it appears that, notwith
standing the statement of Governor Colden, there was
a small sum remitted from the regular charges. It is
evident they got all Colonel Chandler could pay. He
was bankrupt all the rest of his life. For the other
five townships there is every reason to believe that Governor Colden was correct in his statement that full fees
were demanded and received. We have already seen
that Colonel Wells demanded for the New York governor $1,440 for the confirmation of the charter of the
present town of Dummerston. That township was only
a third of the 48,000 acres, called the "equivalent"
lands, and the sum demanded, $1,440, was the full
amount of $90 a thousand acres. After the death of
Governor Moore it is undoubtedly true that some de-

ductions were made from the usual fees but, as the colonial officers were naturally careful to make no record of such deductions, it does not appear just how much they amounted to. Ira Allen, in his history published in London some twenty years later, states that the amount claimed for confirmatory charters was one-half the usual fees.

This statement has been followed by other writers, but there does not appear to be any substantial grounds for it. On the 26th of January, 1773, a petition was made by about four hundred settlers on the east side of the mountains to confirm the titles of the townships in which they were settled for one-half the usual fees of office. This petition was refused. There had then been confirmations of fourteen or fifteen townships. No confirmatory grants were made after the date of that petition. The only confirmatory grants of which any records have been kept, where the township had been settled previous to the application for confirmation, was that of the township of Windsor. It appears from the record of the suit before referred to that Colonel Stone, the agent of the settlers to perfect and procure the confirmation, sold 3,000 acres of land and with the avails of that sale got his confirmatory charter. Of what he received for the land or how much he paid for fees, there is no record. It is not probable, however, that the amount could have been much more than half the regular fees. On the other hand Mr. Knowlton, in behalf of the proprietors of the township of Newfane, went to New York in the winter of 1772, before any settlement had been made on this township, and succeeded in getting a confirmation, not only of the title to the Newfane land, but also of all the franchises in the

New Hampshire charter, including that of the New England town meeting. Mr. Knowlton in the negotiation for that confirmation had the advantage of the New York government. He had not put himself in their power at all; had made no improvements, and, unless he could get a charter on his own terms, was perfectly free to abandon his township. The time of his application was just after the failure of the sheriff of Albany county, with his immense posse, to execute his writ of possession against the Bennington settlers; and it was while Ethan Allen and his Green Mountain Boys were having free scope in their Revolutionary proceedings. It was after they had undertaken to arrest Remember Baker and he had been rescued by ten men within a short distance of where the present city of Troy now stands. In this state of things Mr. Knowlton had probably little difficulty in getting a very liberal deduction from the usual fees. He was a very bright man and fully capable of taking advantage of everything in his favor. If there ever was a confirmatory charter granted for 70 pounds New York money, as stated by Judge Chipman, this was undoubtedly the one. That remission was granted, not in consideration of the hardships of the settlers, but from the conviction that, unless they accepted what was offered, the royal officers would get nothing in the shape of fees, because at that time they could find no speculator who had the hardihood to undertake to buy lands so close as Newfane was to the other settlements. Where the settlers had occupied and made expensive improvements they had put themselves in the power of the government. Their application for the remission of half the fees was refused, because it was believed a greater amount could be extorted from them and that they would yield rather than submit to the risk of losing not only their lands but their improve ments.

# CHAPTER VII.

The decision of the court in those suits at Albany
was followed by vigorous efforts to enforce the judgments, and new judgments were rendered the next
term of that court. Commissioners were sent again to
Mr. Breakenridge's farm to make partition, and they
were met by men making open and forcible resistance.
Several of these men were again indicted at New York
for riot, and one of them, Mr. Silas Robinson, was
arrested and imprisoned for several months. The
sheriff succeeded in executing a writ of possession
against Mr. Carpenter of Shaftsbury, but the tenant he
put in possession found the possession too uncomfort-
able to retain. He did succeed in getting into the
house of Mr. Rose of Manchester, but the neighbors
gathered around in so great numbers that he very
hastily left and directed Mrs. Rose to keep possession
for the claimant, which direction she forgot to obey.
He also attempted to take possession of Mr. Breakenridge's farm, but he was met by armed men, who, in
language not at all ambiguous, told him that if he
persisted in the attempt they would blow out his
brains. Matters had come to such a point that it was
necessary to determine which was the stronger party

And so on the 18th of July, 1771, Sheriff Ten Eyck of Albany gathered the largest *posse comitatus* ever assembled in the province of New York. In that posse were included four lawyers, one of whom had been one of the lawyers for the defendant in the ejectment suits, the mayor of the city, and other high officials. Ira Allen, in his history of Vermont and in the preamble to the Vermont constitution, written by him, states that the number in this force was seven hundred and fifty, and this statement has been frequently copied by subsequent writers. It is very natural to exaggerate the numbers of any body of men, especially those of a hostile force. Governor Hall, quoting from a letter written by Mr. Yates of Albany to Attorney General Kempe and Mr. Duane, fixes the number at about three hundred when it left Albany, with some additions on the way. This statement is probably more nearly correct. The settlers had notice of the approach of this large force and prepared themselves accordingly. They gathered together, as Ira Allen states, to the number of three hundred. But here again the estimate must be too large, because at that time there could not have been three hundred male settlers obtainable within reasonable distance. It does not appear that Baker or either of the Allens were there, and no record is made of the organization that was had. Seth Warner must have been there, and Robert Cochran of Rupert was undoubtedly present. Both of these men, during the Revolutionary War, became colonels in the continental army and developed great capacity and showed undoubted courage as military leaders. A large proportion of the settlers had been soldiers in the French War and were not afraid of the smell of powder. Ira Allen gives some details of a kind of ambuscade that was formed in the woods to meet the attack. From the account given by Mr. Yates, in his letter written the next day, it would seem that the settlers had been arranged in a skillful manner for defense, and had taken advantage of ground and of the cover of the trees. When the sheriff reached the vicinity, he was refused possession of the land. Parleys were had. Mayor Cuyler and Attorney Yates undertook to reason with the settlers; but as it appeared that if they yielded to that reasoning, they would, every one of them, be obliged to give up to the speculator claimants their homes and, in fact, all they had in the world, it is not surprising that they failed to appreciate the reasoning of the mayor and the attorney. The result was, that the negotiations were unavailing and the sheriff gave the order to advance. At this particular period, in the expressive language of Ira Allen, the men composing the sheriff's posse discovered that they had no interest in the matter and refused to advance; and so, without the firing of gun, this large posse retreated. Indeed, it was very wise for them to do so, because, from the courage and fighting capacity shown by these Green Mountain boys a few years later, it is certain the attack could not have succeeded. This was the last attempt to subdue the settlers by any open attack. Frequent applications were afterwards made for regular troops, but the colonial secretary very promptly refused them and stated that troops ought not to be called out in such a contest.

Upon the death of Governor Moore in September, 1769, Governor Colden again succeeded to the government. Shortly afterwards he procured from the colonial council a kind of declaration that they understood the order of Lord Shelburne prohibiting further grants to refer only to those lands that had been included in the New Hampshire charters; and, acting upon that construction, during the time intervening between his taking the office and the arrival of Governor Dunmore in October, 1770, he succeeded in making grants of nearly 600,000 acres of Vermont lands. It is not probable that he succeeded in getting full fees for those grants, but undoubtedly he made them for just what he could get.

The new governor was John Murray, Earl of Dunmore, a Scottish peer, needy and unscrupulous, who had come to this country to amass a fortune; and to that end he was willing to sacrifice every other consideration. His first entry into the colony was marked by an attempt to extort from Governor Colden one-half the fees he had received from land grants after the second of January, the date of Governor Dunmore's commission. Naturally Colden refused to divide, whereupon Governor Dunmore caused a suit to be commenced in the name of the king to compel this division. He had the hardihood to order this suit to be heard and argued before himself as chancellor. Among the Colden papers published by the New York Historical Society is a copy of this bill in chancery and of the answer of Governor Colden and the brief of his attorney, Mr. Duane. Before Governor Dunmore came to the rendition of final judgment he apparently discovered the impropriety of sitting in judgment in his own case and he never rendered the judgment. Although the statement of this extraordinary proceeding seems almost incredible there can be no doubt of its correctness. It is a good illustration of the ignorance and reckless greed of the colonial governors.

Governor Dunmore at once proceeded with the business of granting charters and in so doing utterly ignored the prohibition of the king against granting any lands that had been included in the New Hampshire charters. It is probable that he relied upon the fact that Lord Shelburne and the Chatham administration had been removed and that he expected their high tory successors would overlook his violation of his orders. In this he was disappointed. During his short term of office from October, 1770, to July, 1771, he made grants of between 400,000 and 500,000 acres, every foot of which land was included in the prior grants by New Hampshire. Among these grants was one of 51,000 acres of land in what is now Addison county, embracing parts of Middlebury, Salisbury and Leicester. This patent was issued on the 8th day of July, 1771, the very day on which he surrendered his office to his successor. Five days afterwards every one of those grantees named in that patent conveyed their shares to Governor Dunmore himself.

The order of the king in council prohibiting further grants by the New York government had given great encouragement to the settlers and holders of the New Hampshire patents, and from that date settlers began to come into the grants in considerable numbers. Settlements were commenced in the town of Dorset, in Bennington county, and in the adjoining town of Danby. No sooner had there been considerable improvements begun in these towns than application was made for a New York patent of their lands.

There was a proclamation of the king made in

October, 1763, giving grants of lands to officers and
soldiers of the army who had served in America in the
then late war with France. By these proclamations
field officers were entitled to 5,000 acres, captains to
3,000 acres, subalterns or staff officers to 2,000 acres,
non-commissioned officers to 200 acres, and privates to
50 acres. These grants were to be issued without the
payment of any fees. A large portion of the troops entitled to those patents were disbanded in New York city
and, as they were principally from Europe, were very
ready to dispose of their claims on such terms as were
offered them. Accordingly nearly all of these claims
went into the hands of speculators, just as soldiers'
land warrants in our country were a few years ago
a common subject of speculation. These land warrants
were undoubtedly bought in for small amounts, probably less than the amount of fees for ordinary grants.
At any rate the speculators procured very much the
greatest share of them. After the settlement and
improvements of Dorset and Danby had been commenced, a tract of land called Chatham was granted by
the New York government, nominally to certain soldiers named. This tract embraced 12,750 acres, of
which 10,000 belonged to James Duane. Application
had been made to Governor Colden for this patent, but
he had refused it on the ground that the lands had been
previously granted by New Hampshire. After the
arrival of the Earl of Dunmore as governor, however,
there was no hesitation in granting all that was asked.
This patent was dated March 14, 1771. Another
patent of a tract of 15,350 acres in Rupert and Pawlet,
all of which belonged to Mr. Duane, was granted
June 14, 1771. The settlement of Pawlet had been

commenced about three years previous. That of Rupert was probably commenced in 1770. The settlement of Rutland was commenced in 1770, and of Pittsford about two years earlier. On the 3rd of April, 1771, Governor Dunmore issued a patent for a tract of land, called Socialborough, about six miles wide and extending thirteen miles north and south, embracing 48,000 acres and covering nearly all of the townships of Rutland and Pittsford. The patentees of this patent, a few days afterwards, conveyed their shares to New York speculators, one of whom, James Duane, received conveyance of 15,000 acres. A letter is preserved from his surveyor to Mr. Duane complaining that the settlers on those lands would not permit him to run out the lands included in this grant. This letter was afterwards forwarded by Mr. Duane to the colonial council. If he had believed that the order of that council of May 22, 1765, pretending to forbid the return of any lands in actual occupation of settlers, was intended to be obeyed, he would not have forwarded that letter. From these instances it seems that Mr. Duane had a very keen information of the growth of the settlements, and was very eager to get title covering the lands on which these settlers had made their improvements. And yet Mr. Duane was the man who was instrumental in inserting in the letter of Governor Moore to Lord Shelburne the reference to the order of the New York council of May 22, 1765, prohibiting surveyors from making returns of any lands that were occupied by settlers under the New Hampshire grants. His zeal was very much quickened by the decision of the court at Albany, but after the repulse of the sheriff with his posse at Bennington,

even he seemed to have appreciated the fact that it was
not absolutely certain that he could hold the improved
farms of the settlers. From that date he does not
appear to have taken any more grants of land occupied
by New Hampshire claimants, nor of any other lands,
except a part interest in a patent covering what is now
the town of Clarendon, which he seems to have taken
in combination with some settlers under the Lydius
grant. Mr. Duane took the leading part in favor of
the New York claimants in all their contests against the
Vermont settlers. He was counsel for the plaintiffs in
all the ejectment suits that were brought at Albany.
In a memoir of his life appended to the fourth volume
of the documentary history of New York, it is stated
that he prepared all the arguments to sustain the New
York title that were presented in reports to the New
York assembly during the contests. He also prepared
similar arguments which were presented to the Continental Congress in opposition to the claims of Vermont
for admission to the Union. He was also counsel for
the state of New York in the suit brought by Massachusetts in the federal court to assert its title to lands
within the jurisdiction of New York, and his brief in
that suit appears to be mainly a rehash of his papers
upon the claims of the Vermont settlers. He was
personally interested in the grants of the New York
governors and he seems to have persistently selected
lands that had been occupied and improved. His
biographer states that he had purchased 64,000 acres
of the Vermont lands, for which he had paid $8,000.
That sum was at the rate of 12½ cents an acre which
was more than the actual value of unimproved lands at
that time. He could have got grants of unimproved

lands to any extent for the usual fees of the New York officials which were about nine cents an acre. If he paid the amount claimed, it must have been in the purchase of some soldiers' titles which had been located on improved lands. In the same biography reference is made to a statement of John Adams, that Mr. Duane claimed that his Vermont lands were worth $100,000. If he could have recovered those lands they were undoubtedly worth that amount, because the improvements made by the settlers must, in the aggregate, have been alone worth nearly that sum. If his claim had been legal, it would have been very unjust and oppressive to enforce it. John Adams, who was associated with him in the Continental Congress, records a whining statement of his that he had invested in those Vermont lands almost all his means. He was not entitled to any sympathy on account of the unprofitable result of those investments, neither is the complaint of his biographer that his heirs received in the final settlement only between two and three thousand dollars entitled to any consideration, because he was not, either in law or equity, entitled to anything.

Shortly after his arrival in this country Lord Dunmore was appointed to the government of the province of Virginia. He was so eager to retain his hold on the fees for the New York land grants that he waited until the arrival of his successor before giving up his place.

The successor of Lord Dunmore was Sir William Tryon. He had been governor of North Carolina. Governor Tryon brought with him very explicit instructions prohibiting the grants of any land on the western side of the Connecticut river within the district formerly claimed by the province of New Hampshire. That direction was incorporated into a specific article of the standing instructions to the New York governors numbered "Article 49." This article was laid before the New York council on the 24th of July. Its express terms were:

"It is therefore our will and pleasure that you do take effectual care for the observance of said order in council; that you do not upon pain of our highest displeasure presume to make any grant whatever or pass any warrant of survey of any part of the said land until our further will and pleasure shall be signified to you concerning the same."

Governor Tryon, although professing to be friendly and kind, was in fact artful and treacherous. Mr. Bancroft describes him as the "selfish Tryon, who under a smooth exterior concealed the heart of a savage."

The first grant of lands made by Governor Tryon was 10,000 acres in what was then called Hinsdale, now Vernon, which was granted to a Colonel Howard. It will be remembered that Hinsdale was the western part of a township lying on both sides of the Connecticut river which had been settled by Massachusetts previous to the adjustment of the boundary in 1741. As it was a fractional township the grant of 10,000 acres covered very nearly the whole township. Within it were two forts and near these were settlements which had continued for nearly forty years.

In making this grant Governor Tryon pretended to be governed by an order or, as he termed it, a mandamus from the home government directing him to permit Colonel Howard to select ten thousand acres wherever he chose. He also pretended to have made great efforts to induce Colonel Howard to forbear selecting that land and to have offered him six hundred pounds of his own money if he would desist. These claims were mere pretensions. All the Vermont lands had been withdrawn from any selection by force of the Article 49 just quoted. Instead of being compelled by the order or mandamus of the home government to grant this patent he was expressly and peremptorily prohibited from so doing. There was no order that permitted any selection of improved lands nor of any lands in the actual occupation of adverse claimants. From these facts and the correspondence of the governor with the home government it is certain that he never in good faith offered Colonel Howard six hundred pounds of his own money or any other sum to desist from that selection and his pretense of so doing was only to amuse the settlers and make them believe he was their friend in these transactions. From all the facts of those transactions it would seem that Howard was a "fresh" Englishman who was encouraged by the "ring" around the New York governor to make or pretend to make the selection of that township for the purpose of an experiment to ascertain how far it would be safe to attempt to get possession of the improved lands on the east side of the mountains. His own correspondence which has been preserved is entirely inconsistent with his professions of friendship to the settlers.

Governor Tryon did not succeed, however, in disposing of as much land as his predecessor had. The sturdy resistance made by the Bennington settlers

seems to have abated the zeal of the New York speculators; and, of course, the governor could not sell
unless he could find somebody to purchase. During
the first year of his administration he succeeded in
disposing of about two hundred thousand acres of land
in Vermont in direct violation of his instructions.
Beside other grants he issued a patent of a township of
thirty-two thousand acres by the name of Norbury
in the vicinity of the present towns of Calais and
Worcester. That patent was issued to thirty-two individuals among whom were James Duane, Crean Brush,
Secretary, Banyar, and other noted land speculators.
All these grantees, however, on the second day after
the date of the patent, conveyed their entire interest to
the governor himself. It is a matter of satisfaction
that Governor Tryon made no profit out of this
grant.

During his administration Governor Tryon received frequent letters from the officers of the home
government expressing in unequivocal language their
dissatisfaction with the proceedings of the New York
authorities. On December 3, 1772, the board of trade
made an elaborate report to a committee of the privy
council, reviewing in full the facts in relation to the
New Hampshire grants. This report notices "the
great injury and oppression suffered by the settlers
from the irregular conduct of the governor and council
of New York in granting warrants of survey for lands
under their actual improvements." The report also
notices the exorbitant fees demanded for grants of
lands which are by the ordinance of 1710 "considerably
larger than what are at this day received for the same
service in any other of the colonies." And the report

proceeds to state that the fees exacted at that time by
the governor and other colonial officers were more than
double the amount allowed by the ordinance of 1710
and in many instances were not far short of the real
value of the fee simple. That report also proceeds as
follows: "We think we are justified in supposing that
it has been from a consideration of the advantage
arising from these exorbitant fees that his Majesty's
governors of New York have of late years taken upon
themselves upon the most unwarrantable pretenses to
elude the restrictions contained in his Majesty's instructions with regard to the quantity of land to be
granted to any one person * * * * an abuse
which has now grown to that height as well to deserve
your Lordship's attention."

On the 9th day of the same December Lord Dartmouth wrote to Governor Tryon expressing substantially the same views as those embraced in the report
of the board of trade. He had before that time com-
plained to Governor Tryon of his conduct in granting
lands "annexed to New York by the determination of
the boundary with New Hampshire."

The report of the board of trade and their recommendations for the adjustment of the difficulties were
confirmed by the privy council in the April following.
Among the recommendations for the adjustment of the
difficulty was one that all actual settlers should be
quieted in the possession of the lands they occupied
without regard to the origin of their titles; that the
charters of the New Hampshire townships which had
not been occupied by claimants under New York
should be confirmed to the original proprietors and
those claiming under them without reference to any

subsequent New York patent of the land; and that such subsequent patentees should be indemnified for their loss by grants of other lands. The report had recognized the fact that a positive determination of conflicting claims of lands could only be made by decree of a court or tribunal having jurisdiction and so the order of the king and council approving that report was not in the nature of an order or command but a proposition to the New York government, which, being deemed just and equitable by the king and council, it was hoped would be assented to and carried into execution by that government. This order was communicated by Lord Dartmouth to Governor Tryon with instructions to have it carried into effect. Instead of complying, with these instructions Governor Tryon wrote a long reply insisting that the plan proposed was unjust to the New York patentees and impracticable. The reason why the proposed adjustment was not acceptable to the New York speculators was that it gave those speculators no benefit from the improvements made by the settlers. That proposed adjustment simply gave the speculators other unimproved lands in the place of those included in their New York patents. As has been seen Mr. Duane claimed that his Vermont lands were worth $100,000. The effect of that adjustment would have been to reduce the value of his claims to about $5,000. The real objection of the speculators was that by the proposed adjustment they were prevented from getting an unfair advantage of the settlers. During the correspondence between Lord Dartmouth and Governor Tryon reference was made to the decision of the New York courts which brought out the opinion of Lord Dartmouth above quoted.

## CHAPTER VIII.

### RESISTANCE OF SETTLERS,—A REVOLUTION.

In the meantime settlers were taking active measures to protect themselves. They had no alternative.
If they yielded they must submit to such terms as
were exacted. What would be the nature of those
exactions may be inferred from the demand made by
Colonel Howard of the inhabitants of Hinsdale. His
proposal was that the settlers should lease their lands
for five years at the rent of one penny sterling per
acre; another five years for one shilling per acre, and
at the expiration of that time to come to a new
agreement, which, of course, meant an eviction in case
they declined to comply with whatever terms might be
exacted. In one of his letters to Lord Dartmouth
Governor Tryon states that this offer was "too generous to leave room for complaint." If that was
generous treatment, ordinary or harsh treatment must
have been very much to be dreaded. Upon these facts
the only course left to the settlers was that of resistance. The remainder of the story might be told in
those few words: The resistance was successful and
ended in a revolution.

Shortly after the repulse of Sheriff Ten Eyck the
settlers made their organization for defense. Here
commenced the career which made Ethan Allen famous.

He had great skill in organization, was a man of great personal energy and enthusiasm, and he had the faculty of impressing his associates with the same energy and enthusiasm. During the three or four years that ensued he so perfected the organization of the settlers and so infused into them his own zeal and confidence as to make them the most effective and reliable of all the military organizations in the colonies. Their prowess was such as to justify what was afterwards said of them by General Burgoyne, who, without intending it as a compliment, described them as the most active and rebellious race of people on the continent. Military companies were organized in each settlement. Among the captains of these companies were men who afterwards acquired fame in the Revolutionary War. Such were Seth Warner, who was colonel of the regiment of Green Mountain Boys, Remember Baker, who was killed early in the war, and Robert Cochran, who commanded a New York regiment in the continental army. All these companies were under the command of Ethan Allen with the title of colonel.

These organizations in carrying out the plan of defending their land titles, not only resisted the sheriffs in their attempt to take forcible possession, but also drove off the New York surveyors wherever they were found. They prevented those who had been appointed to office from performing the duties of their office. They also prevented the occupation of any of the New Hampshire grants by settlers under a New York title.

We have seen that in 1744 one Lydius had acquired what was pretended to be a conveyance of a tract of Vermont land, which he claimed had been confirmed by Governor Shirley of Massachusetts. Lydius succeeded in getting some Rhode Island people to take deeds from him. Those purchasers had made some settlements in Clarendon, and perhaps one or two within the present town of Rutland. They very soon found that their Lydius titles were worthless, and further, that there was serious conflict between the New York and the New Hampshire titles. Relying probably on the decision of the court of Albany, they deemed it best to take a New York title, and so they united with Mr. Duane in taking the patent of the tract called Durham. The Vermonters could not permit New York titles to be held in their midst, and they forced these settlers to buy again from New Hampshire. The principal holder of the New Hampshire title was Colonel Willard. He had been connected with the command of Fort Dummer and was interested in the New Hampshire titles of several townships on the east side of the mountains, and of one or two on the west side, and he also held some New York patents. Allen, while requiring these Clarendon settlers to get title from the New Hampshire patentees, at the same time assured them that if Colonel Willard attempted to demand anything more than a fair price for the land without the improvements, he would protect them against that extortion. This was a kind of illegal justice. Most of these Clarendon settlers remained, and became some of the most worthy settlers of the new state. A Colonel Reid got patent of seven thousand acres, covering the present city of Vergennes. He had obtained a warrant of survey as early as 1766 and took forcible possession, driving off a Mr. Pangborn, who had settled on the falls and built a mill. The Green Mountain Boys, as they were termed, restored Pangborn to the possession of his saw mill and pulled down the grist mill built by Reid. Reid's men rallied and retook the place. Allen's men took it back by force, and again pulled down the grist mill and broke up the mill-stones, so they could not be replaced. When the Green Mountain Boys found New York surveyors, they took their compasses and chains away from them and sent them off. If that was not enough, they applied "the beech seal," or, as they sometimes paraphrased it, chastised them with "twigs of the wilderness." Some settlers under the New York patents had the roofs of their houses pulled off. If they were stubborn, they received the "beech seal"; and one of them near Bennington was sentenced to be suspended in a chair on the sign-post of the Catamount tavern. These punishments were usually awarded upon a trial before committees or officers of the Green Mountain Boys; and, in a sort of whimsical bravado, when they had inflicted their punishment, they usually gave their victims a certificate to that effect, knowing very well that these certificates would be carried to the New York officers.

These proceedings were of course illegal and irregular. In short, they were revolutionary. The number of these punishments was not large. Although "the beech seal" has become famous in history and in fiction, there do not appear to have been more than five or six instances of its application; and there were not quite as many instances of interference with the houses of the New York settlers. Of course in a peaceable community, each one of these instances of forcible interference was an outrage against the law·

But there cannot be found another example of a successful revolution and resistance to tyranny, in which there were so few instances of the invasion of ordinary rights. No blood was shed, no property was taken away from its owners, although some was destroyed, and the utmost that was required was, that the people in the community should recognize and respect the rights of the settlers under the New Hampshire titles.

Encouraged by the successful resistance of the Green Mountain Boys to the intrusions of the New York speculators, settlements increased with great rapidity until the breaking out of the Revolutionary War. In 1771 a census was taken of the inhabitants of that part of Vermont on the east side of the mountains, in which it was shown that there were about forty-six hundred people in that part of the state. At the same time on the west side of the mountains there could not have been more than about twenty-five hundred people, making for the whole state about seven thousand people. At the time of the breaking out of the war these settlements had so increased that it is estimated there were then about twenty thousand people in the New Hampshire grants.

These new settlers were largely, if not exclusively, from New England. Salisbury, Connecticut, furnished its full share. It sent Heber Allen to Poultney, Samuel Chipman to Tinmouth, John Chipman to Middlebury, Thomas Chittenden to Williston, Ira Allen to Colchester, besides numerous well known men to other towns. The little town of Tinmouth, which now has hardly one thousand inhabitants, had among its settlers at the outbreak of the war three men, each of whom had one or more sons who were destined to be of great

service to the public and to acquire great honors in the
new state. These men were Samuel Chipman, Samuel
Mattocks and Stephen Royce.

Not only had the number of settlers increased, but
their improvements kept pace with the growth of their
numbers. The settlers of Clarendon built a road
through to Manchester, giving, down through the valley of the Battenkill, communication with Albany. It
is to be noticed that while the settlers revolted from
the government of New York, they did not cease
business relations with the New York people. They
got such supplies as they had largely from Albany, and
it was the boast of the leaders of this revolution, that
they never interfered with the collection of honest
debts due from the settlers.

The Onion River Company commenced improvements in Colchester at what is now Winooski Falls.
Here Remember Baker was employed at his old trade,
building mills. He had already built mills at Arlington and Pawlet, and he finally moved his family to
Colchester. Baker was not only a good mill-wright
and an industrious citizen, but he had been a soldier in
active service in the French war and was one of the
most resolute and active of the partisan leaders in the
fight against the New York authority. Ira Allen,
although the youngest member of the Onion River
Company, having begun operations before he was
twenty-one years of age, became from the start its
leading spirit. He was a man of vigorous intellect,
broad and comprehensive views, good business judgment, and great if not excessive boldness and energy of
action. Under his management the Onion River Company commenced the construction of mills at Winooski,

soon got possession and control of the mills on the
Otter creek, where the city of Vergennes is, and commenced and diligently prosecuted enterprises for the
development of the large real estate that had come into
its control.  The proprietors' records of Colchester
show that the Onion River Company built a road from
Colchester to Castleton.  Of course it could not have
been a very perfect road, and undoubtedly in many
instances it followed roads built by the settlers along
its line.  By these roads there was communication, by
horseback in the summer and sleighing in winter, from
Colchester, by way of Castleton, to Skeensboro, now
Whitehall, and, by way of Clarendon and Manchester,
to Albany.  Other settlers had opened up some of the
towns along the lake shore opposite Crown Point and
Ticonderoga and had begun the usual improvements of
prosperous settlements.

Governor Tryon was entirely helpless against the
opposition of the Vermont settlers.  He applied to the
home government for forces, but received not only a
refusal to grant his application but censure for his
course which had made it necessary.  The sympathies
of most of the people of New York were with the
Vermont settlers.  When complaints were made of
resistance he could only reply by the issue of furious
proclamations, denouncing the settlers as the "Bennington mob" and threatening terrible things against
them.

During the winter of 1772, John Munro, claiming
authority under a New York commission, succeeded in
getting together a force to arrest Remember Baker,
who was then living with his family at Arlington.
This force surprised Baker in his house in the early

morning, wounded him and his wife, and started with them for Albany. Ira Allen stated the number of this force to be fifty. That was undoubtedly an exaggeration of the actual number. Word of this arrest was carried to Bennington and ten men started to the rescue. They succeeded in reaching the Hudson river, at a point where the city of Troy now is, before Munro got there with his prisoners, and so turning towards Arlington they intercepted Munro, who claimed that his men deserted him and ran away. The ten men rescued Baker and his wife from their captors, whatever their number was. The truth of the matter was, that the people of Albany county were in sympathy with the settlers and could not be depended on to carry out any violent measures. Further evidence of this may be noted from the fact that Seth Warner, although one of the most active of the partisan leaders and one for whom large rewards were offered by the New York governor, lived quietly at his home in Bennington within a mile of the New York line without any effort being made to arrest him. Warner was a cousin of Baker, although he had no connection with the land company and does not appear to have been in any sense a land speculator.

In May, 1772, Governor Tryon addressed a letter to the Rev. Mr. Dewey of Bennington, asking that a delegation be sent to New York to confer with regard to a settlement of the difficulties. A delegation was accordingly sent. They were received very graciously by the governor and it was proposed that all prosecutions for the offenses of the settlers in resisting the officers should be suspended until the king's pleasure should be known, and that the governor should recom-

mend to the claimants of the contested lands to put a
stop to all civil suits concerning them. The committee
were pleased with this proposition, and their report
was received at Bennington with great rejoicing; but
to their dismay they learned that, at the very time
these negotiations were proceeding in New York, surveyors in the employ of the New York purchasers were
actively at work, and that Colonel Reid had driven off,
without legal process, the owners of the mills on the
Otter creek, and was himself dispossessed by the
settlers. Each party accused the other of want of
good faith and the pacification was an entire failure.
Governor Tryon issued some more proclamations offering rewards for the capture of leaders and again
applied to the British government for military force.
To this application Lord Dartmouth, on December 9,
1772, made reply, stating his expectation that the
questions which had occasioned the disturbances would
shortly be determined in a manner more effectual to
restore quiet than the interposition of force, which,
he said,

"Ought never to be called into the aid of the civil
authority but in cases of absolute and unavoidable
necessity, and which would be highly improper if applied to support possessions which after the order
issued in 1767 upon a petition of the proprietors of the
New Hampshire townships, may be of very doubtful
title."

During the course of these hostilities elaborate
papers were prepared and submitted to the New York
Assembly, attempting to justify the course of the New
York claimants and to magnify what they termed the
outrages of the settlers or the "Bennington mob."
These papers were usually credited to Mr. Duane.

Beside other claims was one that, on the evening after
the close of the trial at Albany, an interview was had
between the attorney general and others representing
the claimants on the one side, and Ethan Allen and
some of his friends on the other in which it was
alleged that Allen agreed to advise his friends to accept
the situation and make the best terms they could with
the claimants; and it was claimed to be a great breach
of faith on Allen's part that he afterwards refused to
abide by that agreement. It was further claimed that
the resistance of the settlers was due to the influence of
the Rev. Mr. Dewey of Bennington. It is true that
Mr. Dewey was bold and steadfast in his opposition to
the oppression of the claimants, and the people of
Vermont are more largely indebted to him than most
of them are aware for his bold and steadfast course in
the troubles out of which grew the new state. The
statement that Allen agreed to yield was denied by
him and is entirely inconsistent with his well known
traits of character. So far as it is a question of
veracity between Allen and Duane we are bound to
give credit to Allen, because in the whole course of
their proceedings Allen's character for honesty comes
out better than Mr. Duane's. Allen was a boastful
man, indiscreet in his speech, sometimes profane and
not always strictly accurate, but there is nothing in all
his written statements, and he made a great many
of them, to show that he was intentionally untruthful.
On the other hand Mr. Duane's character for honesty
is impeached by an examination of his writings. He is
sometimes found guilty of absolute falsehood, and
frequently guilty of attempts to deceive by concealing
material facts. In the manifesto in question he makes

clamorous complaint against the settlers that they had resorted to violence when they had a perfect remedy by appeal if they had any title to their lands. Mr. Duane was counsel for all the plaintiffs in those ejectment suits and a party in interest in some of them. He knew very well that all the declarations in those suits were intentionally framed so as not to allow any appeal. This statement alone would be sufficient to impeach his veracity. Allen denied ever agreeing to yield or advise the settlers to submit to the decision of the court. It is true that there was an interview between the parties named at a public house in Albany on the evening of the trial. Ira Allen in his history states that at that interview great promises were made to his brother to induce him to give the advice they sought. It must be said, however, that from an interview of the nature of the admitted character of this one, at a public house in the evening after the circulation 'of bibulous refreshments such as would be naturally expected on such an occasion, it would be hardly just to claim that any great question of veracity could arise. It must be confessed that Allen's own statement of his reply that "The gods of the valleys were not the gods of the hills " also seems very much to have the appearance of being more maudlin than heroic.

The New York claimants did not abandon their efforts. Colonel Reid, in the following June, again took forcible possession of the mills on the Otter Creek and established a force of scottish emigrants to take possession for him. In the following August, Allen, Warner and Baker appeared with over one hundred men, and warned the scotchmen to depart, which they

did; and Reid's mill was thoroughly destroyed. Of
course affidavits of these proceedings were sent to New
York and in them it was related that the Green
Mountain Boys conducted in a boisterous manner
and that Baker held up his hand, from which his
thumb had been cut off in his encounter with Justice
Munro, and stated that was his commission. The
same party found Captain Wooster serving ejectment
writs in Addison. They took him and his sheriff and
threatened to apply the beech seal; but, after some
parley, Wooster gave in, sent off his sheriff, and their
treaty of peace was settled over a mug of flip.
Wooster afterwards became a major general in the
Revolutionary army, and was killed during Tryon's
invasion of Connecticut. To this renewed outbreak
Tryon could only reply with more proclamations.
Indeed, his condition was not satisfactory to himself.
He was defied in Vermont, ignored in New York, and
rebuked and repudiated in England, and, what was of
more consequence to him, the stream of fees for new
grants had ceased to flow.

In the winter of 1774 the New York provincial
legislature passed a law, by which it was gravely
enacted that, unless Allen, Warner, Baker, Cochran
and others named in the act, after notice published in
the New York papers, should surrender themselves for
commitment within seventy days, the person neglecting
to surrender himself was "to be adjudged, deemed and
(if indicted for a capital offence hereafter to be perpe-
trated) to be convicted and attainted of felony, as in
cases of persons convicted and attainted of felony
without benefit of clergy"; and the colonial courts
were authorized and directed to award execution

against such offender so indicted for capital offence in the same manner as if he had been convicted or attainted in said courts. It was afterwards claimed by Mr. Duane that this enactment was copied from some old English statutes. There was, however, no statute which furnished a full precedent. If this enactment had not been so ridiculously impotent, it would have been an outrage on all principles of civilized jurisprudence. As it was, it was simply ridiculous. The proscribed parties remaining all the time within the territory claimed to be, and which undoubtedly was, within the civil jurisdiction of the province of New York, defied the law, and, over their own signatures, issued counter proclamations against the New York authorities and speculators, and defied those authorities to come and execute the mandates of that law.

It is related in the "Life of Ethan Allen," by the late Henry Hall, that, after the publication of that proclamation, in which a reward of one hundred pounds was offered for Allen's capture, he boldly rode into the city of Albany in open daylight, went into a public house and called for his drinks, announced his name and the fact of the reward offered for his arrest, and then mounted his horse and rode away. This story seems improbable, but it is by no means impossible to be true. The Vermonters had undoubtedly more friends in Albany than the New York land speculators. In the very next year, after the capture of Ticonderoga and Crown Point, Allen was acting in concert with the New York troops in the invasion of Canada.

It may be noted that one of the principal supporters of this extraordinary enactment was Crean

NEW YORK LAND SPECULATORS.      113

Brush, then holding a seat in the New York assembly
from the county of Cumberland on the east side of the
mountains in Vermont.  The other member of that
assembly from Vermont was Colonel Samuel Wells of
Brattleboro.  As a curious illustration of the fact that
people little apprehend what is in store for them, it
may be noted that within less than ten years after the
enactment of this law the same Ethan Allen married
the step-daughter of Brush, a favorite member of
Brush's family, and, further, that within less than nine
years from that time Colonel Wells, when fleeing for
his life, took refuge in the house of the same Ethan
Allen.

In November, 1772, Governor Tryon communicated to his council information that the settlers had
held a convention at Manchester and had appointed
Jehiel Hawley of Arlington and James Breakenridge of
Bennington their agents to go to England and to apply
to the king for relief against the oppression of the
New York speculators.  When these agents arrived in
London they found their mission had already been
anticipated by the report of the board of trade which
has already been mentioned.  As the recommendations
of that board were satisfactory to them there was
nothing left for them to do but to go home and wait
the action of the privy council on that report.  When
Governor Tryon's reply to that report was received it
became evident that a settlement of the vexed question
was more difficult than had been imagined.  There
were other irregularities of the New York government
in respect to the issue of patents on lands purchased
from the indians.  On account of all these complaints
Lord Dartmouth directed Governor Tryon to come

to England and explain these matters. This direction was given on the 4th of August, 1773. As might naturally be expected Governor Tryon was not especially anxious to meet this investigation and so delayed complying with this direction of Lord Dartmouth until the April following. When he arrived at London there were further delays in the matter of the adjustment of these New Hampshire grants and it was not until the second of March, 1775, that any attempt at an adjustment of these disputes could be made. At that time upon the suggestion of Governor Tryon it was agreed that the case should be stated in New York and carried by a regular appeal to the king and council where there could be an authoritative decision of the whole matter. This of itself would involve a delay of several years. But that delay was not enough to satisfy the New York speculators. The next week an application was made by Colonel Reid to the board of trade for a further delay on the ground that he had further evidence to submit to the board and he wished to have the matter reopened to be heard when Governor Tryon should return from Bath where he was going on account of his health. It would seem that the application for re-hearing before the privy council on the ground of newly discovered evidence, after an interval of eight years from the first application of the settlers, was not a very strong reason for delay. At all events this delay was not upon the application of the settlers nor was it in their interest.

The breaking out of the Revolutionary War prevented any further hearing and Governor Tryon was sent back to New York. Previous to his departure for New York Lord Dartmouth wrote to him on May 4th,

1775, that he would soon be able to send to him the
king's final orders in respect to the matter and further
instructed him as follows :

"In the meantime it will be your duty to take no
further steps whatever regarding those cases and to
avoid, in conformity with the instructions you have
already received, making any grants or allowing any
surveys of locations of lands in those parts of the country which are the seat of the present disputes."

Governor Tryon reached New York June 25th,
on the same day that Washington passed through the
city on his way to take command of the American
army.  In the continental congress a motion was made
for his seizure, but this was opposed by Mr. Duane
and was unsuccessful.  A later attempt was made to
secure him, but it is said that Mr. Duane's footman
was sent to Governor Tryon in season to give him
information of what was resolved and that he escaped
to a man-of-war.  In utter disregard of the parting
instructions of Lord Dartmouth, he issued a patent on
October 26, 1775, for forty thousand acres of land,
and another in June following, . for twenty-three
thousand acres,—both of these patents after he had
taken refuge on board the king's man-of-war.

During Governor Tryon's absence Lieutenant Governor Colden again became the acting governor of New
York.  His official term continued from April 4, 1774,
until June 25, 1775.  During that time he issued
patents for about four hundred thousand acres of
Vermont lands; and in some of those issues he entirely
disregarded his own construction of the king's order,
and sold again lands that he knew had been included in

the grants of Governor Wentworth. It does not seem probable that he could have received the full fees for those patents, which would have been over thirty-six thousand dollars for all the officers. It seems more probable that he took advantage of the situation and issued those patents freely for just what he could get.

During Governor Colden's last administration, the Revolutionary War broke out. On the 10th of May, 1775, Ethan Allen with his Green Mountain Boys made a daring attack on Fort Ticonderoga and took it by surprise with all its armament and munitions of war. On the same day Warner captured Crown Point with its garrison and armament. These occurrences coming after the battle of Lexington filled the friends of the king with astonishment and grief. Governor Colden, then administering the government, a doughty old man of eighty-seven, wrote an account of this misfortune to the british ministry; and in his final statement he unintentionally gave to the settlers of Bennington a compliment, which it will always be their pride to remember. He says "the only people of this province who had any hand in this expedition were that lawless people of whom your lordship has heard much under the name of the Bennington mob." This was the old man's last appearance in connection with the Vermont lands.

It is not the purpose of this paper to follow the story through the Revolutionary War. It is enough to say, that Ethan Allen was taken prisoner and Remember Baker was killed very early in the invasion of Canada. Seth Warner became the principal officer of the Green Mountain Boys in the Revolutionary War

and Robert Cochran became a field officer of one of
the New York regiments in the continental line.
The death of Baker was a great loss to the Vermont
settlers. He was an industrious, good citizen and a
brave and capable soldier.

# CHAPTER IX.

## SETTLEMENTS ON THE EAST SIDE OF THE MOUNTAINS.

While the settlers of western Vermont were having these troubles, those on the east side of the mountains were having a different experience. Although
these settlements were but a few miles distant from
each other, the mountains intervened, and there was
little or no actual communication. In all the town
histories, now so thoroughly collected in the series of
papers commenced by Miss Hemenway, there is no
notice of any communication between the settlers
across the mountains until just before the commencement of the Revolutionary War, when Captain Cochran
with his company of Green Mountain Boys went to
Westminster the second day after the massacre of
March 13, 1775. When Captain Robinson, in November and December, 1766, was making preparations for
the appeal of the settlers to the king, he took petitions
and powers of attorney from nearly a thousand different persons interested in the Vermont settlements.
Those names included nearly every settler on the west
side of the mountains and nearly all the grantees found
in Connecticut, New York and Massachusetts, including
"friend Benjamin Ferris" and the Burlings and
Willises. In that list is found no name of any settler
on the east side of the mountains, nor of any of the

grantees who resided in New Hampshire, nor of those
who held titles to the Connecticut river towns in
Windham and Windsor counties.

At that time the only road across the mountains
was the military road from Charlestown to Crown
Point, passing through what is now the village of
Rutland. That road was made in 1759 and 1760, and
was traversable with wagons from the Connecticut
river to the foot of the mountains and with pack
horses across the mountains to Rutland, but there was
then no road from Rutland to Albany. The shortest
road across the mountains from Bennington to Draper,
now Wilmington, was not made until after 1778, when
its construction was ordered by the state government.
The provincial legislature of New York had ordered a
part of this road in 1774; but their route after
crossing the mountains from the east bore to the south
through Searsburgh and Pownal, for Bennington was
not a pleasant place for New Yorkers to traverse in
those days. There was but little done under this
order, however, for it took about all the taxes raised
in Cumberland county to pay the fees and salaries of
the swarm of officials created by the New York government. In 1771, when Judge Thomas Chandler was
making defense against the removal of the shire of
Cumberland county from his town of Chester, he
stated that, during the preceding year, a route had
been traced from Chester which showed the best pass
within one hundred miles on either side. He stated
that this route could easily be made passable for
carriages, and that there was no other road from
Cumberland county to Albany within one hundred
miles of that pass, except one in Massachusetts over

the Hoosic mountain which he claimed was not a convenient route for travel. It does not appear just when this road from Chester to Manchester was made; but it was for many years the most convenient road across the mountains, and, until the days of railroads, was claimed to be the easiest pass across the mountains south of the valley of the Winooski passing through Montpelier. This was probably the road traversed by Captain Cochran with his company, when he went to Westminster on the occasion of what was termed the Westminster massacre. It was also, as late as January, 1783, the usually traveled road from Brattleboro to Albany, because it was on that road that Col. Wells met the company sent to arrest him. In 1769, when the Deans were arrested in Windsor for cutting pine trees contrary to the requirements of the English charters, the officer having them in charge did not dare to take them through Massachusetts and so took them from Brattleboro across the mountains through the woods, but as there was no road he was obliged to procure a guide.

While the actual distance was much less, there was no road for travel from Albany to those settlements nearer than the one through southern Massachusetts, making the distance about one hundred and fifty miles. This distance was not only great of itself, but it traversed a portion of Massachusetts that was settled by a class of people which would naturally be expected to be hostile to anybody interfering with the settlers on the Connecticut river above the Massachusetts line. Those settlements were largely extensions of Massachusetts settlements from Springfield up the river. The land speculators who had bought the Bennington lands with such avidity could not have anticipated getting possession of the Windham county lands without a struggle with the settlers in possession. In that struggle they would be at a disadvantage, not only from the great distance they would be obliged to travel but also from the hostility they had reason to expect from the settlers of that part of Massachusetts which they would be obliged to traverse. For these or some other reasons there were no purchasers of the improved lands in the New Hampshire grants on the east side of the Green Mountains. As the speculators would not buy, the government officials could not get their fees for patents, unless they could by some means induce the settlers to apply for confirmatory charters. The paramount idea of all the colonial governors of New York was to secure the largest possible amount of fees for land grants. So long as they could get these fees, they were willing to endure insult and defiance in the province and rebuke and censure from the home government. To secure these fees from the settlers on the east side required a very different policy from that adopted with the settlers on the other side of the mountains, and so the history of the two sections of Vermont during those few years shows a most remarkable contrast, not only in the policy of the government but in the experience of the settlers as well. While in case of the settlers of Bennington, who were located within a day's journey of the city of Albany and were isolated from other settlements that sympathized with them by long stretches of mountains without roads, the New York speculators, like Duane, Kempe, Banyer and their associates, were perfectly willing to pay the required fees for patents covering the farms of these settlers, they were not willing to pay those large fees for equally good or better farms in Brattleboro and Putney, distant more than a week's journey from Albany and within easy communication with the settlements of Massachusetts and New Hampshire adjacent, who would be expected to make common cause with their relatives and friends on the Vermont side of the river. To attempt to molest these settlers would be worse than going through a hornet's nest after honey.

The township of Chester had been originally granted by Governor Wentworth under the name of Flamstead and it was regranted in 1761 under the name of New Flamstead. The settlement of this township was commenced in the year 1763 by Thomas Chandler, his two sons and several others from Massachusetts. Chandler was a man of great energy, one of those men peculiarly adapted to pushing settlements, and he very soon began to devise means of making his settlement prosperous. So after the publication in April, 1765, of Governor Colden's order announcing the order of the king making the territory west of the Connecticut river part of the province of New York, Chandler and his associates made a zealous attempt for the establishment of a new county, of which his settlement of Chester should be the county seat. For this purpose he and one of his fellow settlers went to New York to urge that claim. There was good reason for the establishment of the new county, but, although their claim seemed very plausible, they could make but little headway upon their first application. A report was made to the New York council, by a committee of which the historian Smith was chairman, giving specious reasons why the new county ought not to be established. Mr. Chandler and his associates, however, were induced to make application for a New York grant of their township, and from that time on it is wonderful to note the great favor with which all other applications were met. Their new charter was the first one granted by the New York governor after the repeal of the stamp act. It was dated July 14, 1768. Although in the meantime nothing had occurred to avoid the objections of the committee, a law was speedily passed by the colonial legislature creating the new county of Cumberland, making Chester its county seat. Two days after the new charter of the town, commissions were issued making Thomas Chandler chief judge of the court of common pleas, surrogate and justice of the peace; John Chandler, clerk of the courts; Thomas Chandler, Jr., justice of the peace and quorum; Nathan Stone, of Chester, high sheriff of the county, and Timothy Olcott, coroner. It was certainly a generous crop of officials for a new town. In addition to this, Chandler had, early in the same year, been made colonel of a militia regiment organized in the southern part of that county. For some time, as may be expected, these new officials were zealous advocates of the New York jurisdiction. It must be confessed, however, that after the removal of the county shire from Chester to Westminster and the appointment of Crean Brush as clerk of the court in place of John Chandler, in 1772, the zeal of the Chandlers very seriously abated and Thomas Chandler, Jr., became an early adherent to the new state of Vermont, in which he was advanced to many high offices.

The next township to be rechartered was Brattleboro. It will be remembered that this was one of the three towns formed out of the forty-eight thousand acres of "equivalent lands" sold by the state of Con-

necticut. Of this town Colonel Samuel Wells was an
early settler. He had taken up a farm of six hundred
acres just east of where the present village of Brattleboro is, on part of which some of the grounds of the
present Vermont insane asylum are situated. He was
said to be wealthy and was, a prominent and active
man in the new settlement. In the next year, as appears from the letter of the agent of the heirs of Governor Dummer already referred to, he was found to be
an agent of the New York government to procure the
settlers of Dummerston to apply for a confirmatory
charter. Colonel Wells was throughout the whole contest an active supporter of the New York claimants,
was appointed one of the judges of the New York courts
and was by the New York party made one of the representatives to the colonial assembly. He was one of the
men who, in 1771, made an affidavit that there were
not over one hundred families in all the grants between
the mountains and the Connecticut river in 1765. He
was one of the men in that county on whom the New
York authorities chiefly relied. When he died shortly
after the Revolutionary War, although he had been reputed wealthy and had lived in considerable style for a
frontier settler, it was found that he was bankrupt and
his estate was owing some $15,000 more than the value
of all his property, which was a large sum for those
times, and that his creditors were mainly the same
New York speculators with whom the settlers on the
other side of the mountains had their troubles. There
is satisfaction in thinking that Col. Wells made these
speculators pay well for his assistance in those contests
with the settlers under the New Hampshire titles.
Whether his influence had anything to do with the

application for the confirmatory charter of Brattleboro
is purely a matter of conjecture.

The title to the lands of Brattleboro was one
which must have been held good in any honest court.
The most of that township was within the undoubted
limits of the charter of Massachusetts, for the line of
Massachusetts running west from the point three miles
north of the most northerly bend of the Merrimac
river, described in that charter, even as claimed by
New Hampshire, would cross the Connecticut river
near or above the north line of Brattleboro. That
charter was a proprietary charter and by it there was
given to the province of Massachusetts just as good a
right to sell lands in Brattleboro as in Springfield or
Northhampton. Massachusetts had sold these lands to
Connecticut; Connecticut had sold them to the syndicate of which Colonel Brattle and Governor Dummer
were members; and Governor Wentworth had given a
confirmatory charter to the settlers under the old title.
Such considerations as these had, however, no weight
with the New York governors against their greed for
fees. On the other hand, this was the township in
which Fort Dummer had been built, and some parts of
the town had been settled more than forty years. The
improvements made during such long settlements were
worth much more than the amount of fees exacted and
the timid proprietors could not afford to take any risk
in delaying to apply for a confirmatory charter.

The next township to be rechartered was Hert-
ford, now Hartland. That was a tract of land of
better than ordinary quality. It lay on the Connecticut
river, a stream navigable for all purposes of the early
settlers, and this gave settlers there great advantage

over those of the interior townships. It had settlements with considerable improvements and its great meadows were too valuable to permit any risk of losing their title. The same considerations applied to Putney, the next in the order of application for new charters. Confirmatory charters were granted to Townshend and Tomlinson, now Grafton, the next year. These, together with a tract of five thousand acres in what is now the town of Athens, were all the charters issued during the lifetime of Governor Moore.

The act creating the new county of Cumberland was returned by the king with his disapproval. Mr. Davis, in his History of Cumberland County, seems to consider it strange that this act should be disapproved. While the creation of a new county for the accommodation of the settlers was not only a reasonable but a very necessary act, the details of that law gave abundant reason for its disapproval. Among its provisions was one to the effect that all lands held under charters from the government of New Hampshire should continue to remain within the county of Albany. This extraordinary provision would make the new county cut up like squares on a checkerboard and leave most of its settlers still within the county of Albany,—a provision which would entirely defeat the beneficent purpose of the establishment of the new county. The object of this extraordinary provision was too apparent. It was for the purpose of providing that all trials of the title to lands in dispute should be had at Albany. The framers of that bill were unwilling to allow those cases to be heard before the jurors of the county. There was another objection to the provisions of that bill, which seems to have been

the one named in the disapproval. That disapproval
very seriously deranged the operations of the New
York governor in the new state. Not discouraged,
however, the colonial governor and his council by an
ordinance, as it was termed, re-established the county
of Cumberland early in 1768, and upon that re-estab-
lishment the officers under the first organization were
re-appointed, except the sheriff. Stone, who appears to
have moved from Chester to Windsor. The settlers,
however, did not accept this ordinance with entire
respect. Knowing that the first law creating the new
county had been disapproved by the king, they saw no
reason why the second ordinance should not meet the
same fate. Indeed, the establishment of a new county
by the ordinance of the governor and council was, to
say the least, an act of very questionable validity.

There were several causes of dissatisfaction among
the settlers. All the principal officers of the county
were appointed by the governor and council. This
was inconsistent with the yankee idea of electing their
own officers in town meeting. Although no settler was
evicted on account of the New York title there was a
steady pressure to persuade them to pay large fees for
the confirmatory titles. This was exceedingly dis-
tasteful. The great number of offices created for the
county, including seven or eight judges of the courts,
the surrogate and coroner, numerous justices of the
peace and the quorum, all of whom managed to get
something out of the county, either in fees or salaries,
made the county administration an expensive luxury.
Large jury service was required at the terms of court,
which was burdensome. The fees allowed against
debtors in actions in the courts were large and oppres-

sive. In all these respects the condition of the settlers on the west side of the river compared very unfavorably with that of their neighbors in New Hampshire. The whole population of the county was only about 4,000 and the number of officers supported by that county would be burdensome to a county ten times its size. There was undoubtedly, in addition to all this, a turbulent element, to whom even an honest administration of justice was very offensive.

When the officers of the new county undertook to perform their duties, they were openly resisted and defied. The leaders of this resistance resided in Windsor. At their head was Colonel Nathan Stone. When the sheriff undertook to make an arrest, they resisted him and rescued the prisoner. For this they were naturally prosecuted. The names of the parties who were so prosecuted included a number of men who afterwards became leading citizens of the new state, and they are familiar names in the later history of the northern part of the state. General Benjamin Wait, the founder of the town of Waitsfield, was one of them. When the time for holding the term of court came on, these Windsor men appeared, with Col. Stone at their head, and Stone, with a drawn sword, objected to the proceedings, forced the court to dismiss the actions against the men prosecuted for riot and resistance, and, in fact, broke up the term of the court. They made prisoner of a man named Grout, who had settled at Chester, and who, although not regularly admitted to the bar was trying to get a living out of his practice, or rather his practices, as a lawyer. He was very offensive to these Windsor people who took him prisoner, carried him to Windsor, and detained him

for several days, trying to force him to give up his
law business. After a while he escaped, went to
New York with his complaints and commenced civil
and criminal prosecutions against Stone and his associates. These prosecutions must have given the
New York government considerable uneasiness. It
was not strong enough in that county to subdue the
offenders. The colonial officers dared not attempt to
take their prisoners over the mountains, nor through
Massachusetts to Albany, and their own disregard of
the express orders of the home government prevented
their seeking assistance from that source. Whatever
may have been the reasons for that action, the prosecutions against Stone and his associates seemed to have
been mysteriously dropped, and Stone, instead of being
a rebellious opponent of the New York authority,
turned up as an applicant for a recharter of the town
of Windsor. He was appointed to several offices in
the county, and finally, after the establishment of the
state government, his adherence to the New York
authority was so strong as to cause him to make some
indiscreet remarks against the authorities of the new
state, for which he was promptly arrested and fined.
He was admitted by the colonial government of New
York into the inner circle and made one of the
grantees of some Vermont lands in the northern part of
the state.

During the next year application was made by the
proprietors of several townships, setting forth the
hardships of the new settlement and the uncertainty
hanging over the titles to their lands by which they
were made unsalable, and requesting that they might
be allowed confirmatory charters for one-half the usual

fees. This application was rejected. From that time
it would seem to have been the policy of Governor
Tryon to insist in each case on as large fees as the
applicants could be induced to give.

In 1771 the settlers of the towns along the Connecticut river made application for the removal of the
shire to some town on the river, and Westminster was
in 1772 designated for the new shire of the county.
Among the applicants for this change Colonel Wells of
Brattleboro and Colonel Stone of Windsor were prominent.  At about the same time Crean Brush, who had
been connected with the New York government in the
office of the clerk of the council and who had large
investments in the grants made by Governor Colden of
the Bennington county lands, came to Westminster and
located there as an attorney.  He is said to have been
the first resident attorney in the state of Vermont,
although his settlement in the county was subsequent
to that of Grout and other names appear on the records
as appointed attorneys.  When Brush came to the
county he was at once appointed clerk of the courts.
The record shows that he was appointed clerk in
the place of John Chandler "removed for misconduct."
What that misconduct was, unless it was holding an
office that some favorite of the governor wanted, is not
shown by the record.  Brush took a leading part in
the affairs of the new county, and when, in 1773,
there was an election of members of the colonial
assembly, he and Colonel Wells were returned as members from Cumberland county.  Not much is known
about that election.  Mr. B. H. Hall in his history
shows a bill that was presented against Wells for
" nessosnrces " furnished during that election at Halifax.

From this it would seem that the election had proceeded according to the modern system.

During that time the number of terms of the court was doubled, so as to make four terms a year. This aggravated the burdens of the settlers. There was a continuous and growing discontent. The people of that county held several meetings, in which were discussed, not only the grievances occasioned by the English government which resulted in the Revolution, but also their own special grievances. They sent to the colonial legislature numerous applications for relief, which were either ignored or denied; and they also sent, in common with a great number of others in the province, a written request to the colonial legislature to join the other colonies in concerted measures for their protection against the encroachments of the home government. That legislature, however, was entirely controlled by the tory element.

Early in March, 1775, application was made to Judge Chandler and the other judges to omit the coming term of court set for the 14th of March. Chandler gave some encouragement, but his language was ambiguous. A large number of the citizens of the county who favored measures for relief of the settlers assembled at Westminster on Monday. In the evening the sheriff gathered together a number of the tory element. The whigs took possession of the court house, determined that no court session should be had the next day. Relying upon the promise of Judge Chandler that no armed force should attack them, they had no fire arms and no other weapons than sticks from the wood pile. At midnight the sheriff attacked the court house with a posse of men, fired upon those in sight, killed two and

wounded several others. This was what is termed the
"Westminster Massacre." Its effect was, however,
utterly to destroy the royal authority and, in fact, to
overturn the authority of the province of New York in
that county. Upon news of that massacre the citizens
of the surrounding towns gathered together, like the
rally of the clans of the scotch highlanders described in
the Lady of the Lake. Men came from all parts of
Cumberland county and from across the river in New
Hampshire, and a swift express was sent across
the mountains for Captain Robert Cochran with his
company of Green Mountain Boys. They came as
swiftly as any available means of travel could bring
them; and there was nobody there more eager for the
fray than were those Green Mountain Boys. Captain
Cochran took great pleasure in reminding these New
York officers that a large reward was offered for his
own capture, and invited them to take him and claim
their reward.

It required the utmost efforts of the cooler men of
that crowd, like Colonel Bellows of Walpole, New
Hampshire (from whom we have the name of Bellows
Falls), to prevent the excited crowd from taking sum-
mary vengeance upon the judges and officers of the
court. As it was, they were arrested and taken under
guard to Northampton, Massachusetts, where they
were lodged in jail, and Captain Cochran and his company had great pleasure in being part of that guard.
These prisoners were, as a matter of course, removed
to New York on habeas corpus proceedings and released
by the colonial government. The more exciting scenes
of the American Revolution which soon followed pre_
vented any further action in this contest. Governor

Colden, in making his report to the home government, was very careful to state that the causes of this outbreak were not the same as those upon which the west side settlers had acted. He stated that no settlers had been evicted on a New York grant nor disturbed in the occupation of his land. This was true, but, on the other hand, the fact that the settlers of Bennington had been so disturbed and that chief justice Livingston, who had presided at the trial of those Bennington cases, had also come to Westminster and presided at at least one term of that court, had rendered the settlers very uneasy in the fear that their turn would come. The attempt of Colonel Howard upon the settlers of Hinsdale was not forgotten. While he had brought no suits and attempted no force, he had still been there and had threatened great things. He was without doubt encouraged by Governor Tryon to make the attempt upon the settlers, at the same time that Tryon himself was professing to be the friend of the settlers and pretending that he only acted in obedience to orders from the home government. As Mr. B. H. Hall says, the settlers believed Tryon was their friend in that transaction. He had pretended to have offered Howard six hundred pounds out of his own pocket to surrender that patent. He never paid a penny for that purpose and the records now show that while he was professing this great friendship for the settlers he was writing to the board of trade that the terms Colonel Howard offered the settlers were "so generous as to leave no cause for complaint."

All these things and the efforts made to induce the settlers to pay the big fees for confirmatory grants tended to make them uneasy and more ready to join the other colonies in their resistance. When Governor Colden claimed that the Westminster outbreak was the result of the contagious example of the people of Massachusetts, he stated only part of the real cause. The whigs of Cumberland county were actuated by the same motives as their Massachusetts neighbors. They had as additional reasons the oppressions by the New York government of Cumberland county; and those who had not taken their confirmatory titles were further stimulated by the fear that they would sooner or later be called upon to make the same defense to their land titles as had been made by their Bennington neighbors.

## CHAPTER X.

### ORGANIZATION OF STATE GOVERNMENTS.

The breaking out of the Revolutionary War so occupied the attention of all parties that for some years the contest with New York was ignored. In the meantime a large portion of the purchasers of the New York titles had joined the enemy and their land interests had been confiscated. A state government was organized for New York in the year 1777. During the same year an independent government was organized for Vermont. At the organization of that government Thomas Chittenden was made governor and Ira Allen was a member of the council. While Ira Allen held no great position in name, he was in fact the guiding spirit of that government; and his skill and energy, tempered by the practical judgment of Governor Chittenden, carried the new state through difficulties that would have crushed a less able administration.

When the New York state government was organized George Clinton was made governor. His government should not be confounded with that of the colonial governor Admiral Clinton. The new governor, George Clinton, was a member of one of the leading colonial families of New York. He was thoroughly imbued with the aristocratic sentiments of those times

and had some small interests in the Vermont lands
under some of the grants of Governor Colden. The
constitution of the state of New York was adopted on
the 8th of May, 1777. By it the validity of all grants
made by the colonial government of that province was
affirmed. This provision annulled all the New Hampshire titles and that annulment was made part of the
organic law of the state. At the same time a claim
was made to all quit rents accruing upon land grants
that had been made in the name of the king within the
province. This was of itself a very unjust provision.
Its effect would be to put most of the burdens of the
state government upon these lands, for the largest portion of the land grants of New York had been made
upon merely nominal quit rents.

The good conduct and activity of the Green
Mountain Boys in the military operations of 1777
attracted the favorable notice of the whole country.
Even the legislature of New York was induced to consider the claims of the Vermont settlers. Previous
to that time they had denounced those claims as unjust
and iniquitous and as made upon frivolous pretenses.

In February, 1778, a joint committee of the senate
and assembly of that state was appointed to take into
consideration "the unhappy situation of the good sub-
jects of the state in the eastern district." This committee made a report recommending the adoption of a
series of resolutions, with a preamble containing a
recital of the grievances of the settlers. This preamble
recited that among the causes of disaffection were the
high quit rents reserved in the land grants of New
York, the exorbitant fees of office demanded by the
colonial officials for confirmatory charters, the fact that

"the interests of the servants of the crown and of new adventurers were in many instances, contrary to justice and policy, preferred to the equitable claims for confirmation of those who had obtained the lands under New Hampshire or Massachusetts Bay," and further that this disaffection had been greatly increased by the outlawry enactments of the colonial legislature. The resolutions adopted contained provisions for reducing quit rents to the same amount reserved in the New Hampshire charters. This was, of course, a relief. They further provided for the repeal of the acts of outlawry. This was of no effect because by their own limitation they had expired two years before. They further provided that confirmatory grants should be made to the settlers under the New Hampshire charters upon the payment of small patent fees. This provision was however so carefully drawn as to limit this confirmation to such lands as were possessed by the settlers at the time the grants of them had been made by New York. This provision, if it had been valid, would exclude the greater part of the inhabitants on the west side of the mountains from its benefits. These resolutions and the proposals were made known by the proclamation of Governor Clinton on the 23rd of February, 1778. This proclamation was very plausible upon its face and has been regarded by some modern writers as a generous offer on the part of New York. Colonel Stone, in his life of Brant, speaks of that proclamation as conceived in the most liberal spirit and of the resolutions themselves as offering to confirm all the titles which had previously been in dispute. Mr. B. H. Hall describes them as "such overtures to the disaffected inhabitants of the northern counties as were

deemed compatible with the dignity of New York as a
state and with the welfare of those with whom a
reconciliation was desired." To the settlers themselves
the dignity of the state of New York was of much less
importance than that they should be allowed to occupy
what was in justice their own property. These resolutions offered no security to the settlers. No principle
of law is better established than that it is not within
the power of a state legislature to retake property
that had previously been legally conveyed by any competent authority. The New York grants of lands
covered by the New Hampshire charters had been
declared valid by the colonial courts and that decision
had been incorporated into the constitution and organic
law of the state of New York. It was thus entirely
out of the power of the New York legislature to confirm any of these New Hampshire grants.

Shortly after his return from captivity, Ethan
Allen published a reply to the proclamation of Governor Clinton in which he pointed out in vigorous terms
the entire insufficiency of these proposals. Had they
been accepted by the settlers and the government of
New York established there was no power that could
have prevented Mr. Duane from recovering the full
$100,000 worth of property which he claimed under
those grants and which, according to the memoir already
referred to, consisted in improvements made by the
settlers to the value of $92,000 and $8,000 paid
by him for his claims. Allen's paper contains this
paragraph:

"From what has been said on this subject it
appears that the overtures in the proclamation set
forth are either romantic or calculated to deceive woods

people, who in general will not be supposed to understand law or the powers of legislative authority."

It is however undoubtedly true that these plausible offers did make an impression upon those "woods people" and that Allen's vigorous exposition of their fallacy was by some of the Vermont parties treated lightly because he was himself a land speculator. This reply of Allen was published in August and it had the effect to draw from the New York legislature and Governor Clinton further proposals, among which was one declaring that, as each case must be determined according to its particular merits, it was proposed to submit each case "to such persons as the Congress of the United States should select or appoint for that purpose"; and it was further proposed that those cases should be decided according to equity and not according to strict rules of law. This was very plausible but entirely ineffectual, because the legislature had no power to submit the rights of persons who had bought land under titles declared valid by the constitution of the state, to the arbitration of anybody except the regularly appointed tribunals of the state. Much less had they power to waive any rights which those purchasers had under the rules legally applicable to their claims. This second proclamation did not seem to have as much influence upon the "woods people" as the first.

The organization of the new state of Vermont was interrupted by the excitement occasioned by the British invasion under General Burgoyne. The affairs of the new state were for a time committed to the care of what was termed the "council of safety." This council was confronted at the outset with a lack of means to

conduct any defensive operations. This difficulty was
however obviated by a scheme, of which Ira Allen was
the author, for the confiscation of the property of those
residents who had declared their adhesion to the royal
government and had sought protection from the in-
vading army. So promptly was this plan carried out
that a regiment was raised and equipped within about
a month. Although the other states adopted similar
plans during the Revolutionary War, this was the first
instance of any such action; and Allen claimed the
credit of being the originator of a plan that was afterward generally adopted. When the new state government was organized the sale of confiscated property
became the principal source of its revenue. Its affairs
were managed with great economy and those funds
were sufficient to keep the state finances in good condition for several years.

When this state government was first established
a very considerable portion of what was then termed
Cumberland county adhered to the jurisdiction of New
York. Committees of safety in the interest of New
York were appointed but they did not have power to
enforce any of their orders. The town of Guilford
was then, and remained for many years afterwards,
the most populous town in Vermont, and although it
was divided in sentiment the majority was usually
found to be in favor of the New York jurisdiction;
and so at first was the majority of the inhabitants of
Brattleboro and Halifax and some other towns on that
side of the mountains. The state government of Vermont was, however, administered with such energy
and wisdom as fully asserted its authority, while at the
same time the punishments for resistance to that au-

thority were not severe. The leaders of the resistance were promptly arrested and taught that it was unsafe to trifle with the new state government. To all these proceedings Governor Clinton had nothing to oppose but proclamations. It would seem that the governors of New York, both colonial and state, had taken pattern from the example of their illustrious predecessor, Peter Stuyvesant, who, according to the Knickerbocker History, was the discoverer of the art of conducting governments by proclamation.

# CHAPTER XI.

Early in the history of the new state government came up the question of the disposition to be made of the ungranted lands in the state. During the session of 1779, the legislature formulated plans for the manner of making new grants. They were very much like those adopted by Governor Wentworth of New Hampshire and were similar to those followed in most of the New England states. By these plans were to be formed townships of about six miles square with the New England system of township government, including the town meeting. The lands were to be granted in about seventy rights in each township, of which five were to be public rights, one for the support of a college, one for the benefit of a county grammar school, one for an english school, one for the first settled minister and one for the support of preaching. That would leave about sixty-five proprietary rights for each township. During that session the legislature disposed of a number of townships of land that had never been covered by any grants either from New York or New Hampshire. In disposing of these lands they managed to secure as grantees many prominent inhabitants on the east side of the mountains and in fact some who had been inclined to support the jurisdiction of New York.

At the same session Ira Allen was appointed agent of the state to visit the legislatures of neighboring states and distribute certain pamphlets that had been prepared in defense of the action of the settlers in organizing the new state and justifying their resistance to the New York speculators. In addition to these duties which were pointed out in the record it appears that he was also entrusted with the duty of procuring purchasers for the vacant lands of the state and furnished with blank petitions for distribution among the people he should visit.

As is apparent from the sequel Allen very successfully performed this last duty, for at the October session of the legislature for 1780 were found applications for grants of new townships upon which were issued during that session the charters of about fifty towns. In procuring these petitions Allen not only found men who would pay the charter fees in hard money, but men whose influence would be of great value to the new state. In short he managed to put these lands "where they would do the most good." Among the applications for these new charters were found the names of Colonel Timothy Bigelow of Massachusetts, to whom was granted the township of Montpelier; Colonel Ebenezer Crafts of the same state, to whom was granted the township named for him, Craftsbury; General John Glover of Marblehead, Massachusetts, who had been distinguished in the Revolutionary War, to whom was granted the township of Glover; Commodore Abram Whipple, to whom was granted the township called Navy, so named in recognition of the naval services of the grantee in the war; Major Buell of Coventry, Connecticut, to whom was

granted the township of Coventry; Major Woodbridge,
to whom was proposed to be granted the township of
Woodbridge, but which grant was never perfected ;
Dr. Arnold of Providence, Rhode Island, who was a
member of the continental congress, to whom was
granted the township first named Providence, now
known as Lyndon, and who afterwards became the
grantee of the neighboring townships of St. Johnsbury
and Kirby; and also General William Barton of Providence, Rhode Island, to whom was granted the township now bearing his name. These and other less
noted names were found among the grantees of those
fifty townships. A fact worthy of notice in the same
connection is that none of these applications for grants
were by "dead heads," but every one making them paid
or agreed to pay in hard money the charter fees fixed
by the governor and council. The amount of these
fees varied in each town. They were usually from
seven to ten pounds, New England currency, for each
right ; and, as the rights were supposed to be of about
three hundred and thirty acres each, the cost of those
lands would, in round numbers, be about as many
cents per acre as there were paid pounds granting fees
for each right. That would make the purchase price
of the lands from seven to ten cents per acre, which
was a little less than the charter fees demanded
by the New York colonial governors. Moreover
the value of those lands must have increased between the time of the colonial grants and the state
grants, and the state grants were unincumbered with
any quit rents or reservations of timber for the royal
navy, which were serious objections to the colonial
grants. On the other hand these applications were

procured during the Revolutionary War when money and especially hard money, was very scarce and when the title proffered by the state government could not have been under the circumstances very good. But every additional proprietor that could be found strengthened the influence in favor of the new state. General Washington in speaking of this fact in a letter written two or three years later used this language :

"'They have a very powerful interest in these New England states and pursued very politic measures to enlarge and increase it long before I had any knowledge of the matter and before the tendency of it was seen into or suspected; by granting upon very advantageous terms large tracts of land in which I am sorry to find the army in some degree have participated."

There was in those times no keener observer of current events nor any man of sharper business sagacity than General Washington. The "politic measures" referred to were the work of Ira Allen.

## CHAPTER XII.

Numerous applications were made to the continental congress for the recognition of Vermont as an independent state. Of course this was strenuously opposed by the New York government; and the settlers again found their old enemy, Duane, in their way. The services of the Green Mountain Boys in the Revolution had made a favorable impression on the country. The result was a feeling not only of friendship towards the Vermonters but of respect for their prowess. It had become apparent that the men who had fought at Hubbardton and Bennington were not to be despised in any other contests in which they should engage. The continental congress was however too weak and timid to take any decided action against the protests of New York.

The question of land titles, although not so prominently named, was really the most serious obstacle to the adjustment of the controversy between New York and the new state. If the jurisdiction of New York was confirmed, then all titles to lands in Vermont would be settled by New York courts; and the settlers very well knew how little they had to hope for and how much to fear from these courts. If the jurisdiction of the new state was established, they had reason to expect those titles would be passed upon by courts which were, to say the least, not prejudiced against the settlers nor hostile to them. During the years 1779 and 1780 resolutions were passed by congress tending to favor the New. York claim. In the meantime both New Hampshire and Massachusetts had set up claims to the territory of the new state and the government of Vermont had got itself into difficulties by favoring the applications made by some towns in New Hampshire near the Connecticut river and also by some towns in New York east of the Hudson river for a union with the new state. In September, 1780, a hearing was commenced before the continental congress in which New York and New Hampshire were admitted as parties claimants. Ira Allen and Stephen R. Bradley were present in behalf of the new state. Finding themselves ignored in the hearing Mr. Allen and Mr. Bradley on the 22nd day of September withdrew their appearance in a spirited letter giving their reasons in detail.

These applications of the new state for admission to the Union and the refusal of congress to accept them, as might well be supposed, did not fail to attract the attention of the British authorities. The correspondence of General Haldimand, the governor of Canada, with the home government, has been published, and shows that, as early as 1778, the British officers were carefully watching that action. In 1780 Beverly Robinson of New York, a noted royalist or tory as he was commonly called, wrote a letter to Ethan Allen, proposing negotiations with the view of detaching Vermont from the confederacy. No notice was taken of this letter which was received by Allen some time

during that summer.   In the winter of 1781 Mr. Robinson wrote another letter to Allen.   Copies of this
letter and of the preceding one were forwarded on the
9th of March to the president of congress with a letter
in Allen's characteristic style, asserting that inasmuch
as congress had rejected their application for a union
the people of Vermont had a perfect right to negotiate
with the British or any one else.

   During the summer of 1780 application was made
to Governor Haldimand for an exchange of prisoners,
some of the inhabitants of Vermont having been taken
captives in some forays across the border.   Ira Allen
in his history states that this application was for the
release of prisoners taken in the raid upon Royalton,
but as this raid was not made until some months after
the application of Governor Chittenden, Allen's memory was at fault.   A flag was received and upon that
application a truce was arranged between Ethan Allen,
commanding the Vermont militia, and the British
troops then holding possession of Lake Champlain.
Commissioners for the exchange of prisoners were
received within the British lines and the British authorities manifested a very kindly spirit towards the
Vermont officers.   In addition to other business with
regard to exchange of the prisoners there was undoubtedly a great deal of conversation in respect to a
proposition to make Vermont an independent British
province.   This negotiation was mainly carried on by
Ira Allen.   He very adroitly declined to commit himself in writing, for the obvious reason that if any such
writing should fall into other hands than those for
whom it was intended it would very seriously compro-
mise him and embarrass the whole negotiation.   These

negotiations were continued until the close of the war. It is not the purpose of this paper to enter into a detailed discussion of those negotiations or of the merits or demerits of the principal actors in them. There is an abundance of discussion on this topic.

The existence of this truce and the sending of commissioners for the avowed purpose of exchanging prisoners did not escape the attention of the New York government. Indeed it is more than probable that it was the intention of both the Allens to conduct that business in such a way that it would be discovered by the New York authorities. The correspondence of General Schuyler and Governor Clinton shows that they were aware of these negotiations and were suspicious of what has since been shown were undoubtedly the real negotiations. In the meantime General Haldimand had communicated the facts to the home government, and a letter of Lord George Germaine, colonial secretary, to Sir Henry Clinton, was found in a captured vessel in which he stated that the return of Vermont to the british allegiance was an object of great importance and stating that he had given directions to General Haldimand to do what he could, etc. This letter was published in the Philadelphia papers on the 4th of August. It seems to have attracted the very decided attention of congress. It is to be remembered that in the early part of the year 1781 the cause of the colonists seemed more hopeless than ever before. In order to avert the danger of the defection of Vermont very prompt measures were taken by congress. On the 7th of August a resolution was passed inviting the authorities of Vermont to send their agents to confer upon a plan for the admission of Vermont into

the confederacy. Accredited agents of Vermont for
that purpose were very speedily appointed. In fact
they were already on hand and the business was con-
cluded by the adoption by congress of a resolution on
the 20th of August in substance, that if the state of
Vermont would accept as its boundary the line of
Connecticut river on the east and that of 20 miles
east of the Hudson river on the west it should be
admitted into the confederacy. This was, without
doubt, exactly the result sought for by the Vermonters
in those negotiations.

From all the evidence, taken in connection with
the acknowledged facts which show what the actual
interest of the parties was, there can be no doubt that
the actors in this negotiation as well as the settlers of
the new state were unanimous in their preference for
an independent state organization admitted to the confederacy on equal terms with the other states. This
choice was not concealed in any of the correspondence
and was perfectly apparent from all the facts of which
the british authorities were keeping such careful watch.
On the other hand, when it came to be a question
whether Vermont should be included in the confederacy
as a part of the state of New York or become an
independent colony even under the control of the
british crown, it cannot be denied that the interest of
most of the active men in this negotiation was against
the New York jurisdiction.

The establishment of the jurisdiction of New York
meant a great deal to those men. It involved the loss
to them of every piece of property either of them had
in the world. It appears that eight men besides Allen
were from the first in the secret of Allen's negotiations

with Governor Haldimand. This was the statement of
Governor Chittenden to Mr. Williams in 1793, as
appears from his history, and is shown by the written
signature of those men to a paper given to Ira Allen at
the time. Of these men, six lived in the town of
Bennington and one in Sunderland. Another was Governor Chittenden who had a temporary home in
Arlington during the war but whose permanent home
and property interests were in Williston and Jericho.
The homes of every one of these Bennington men
were, with all their buildings and improvements, either
actually covered by judgments in ejectment in favor of
the New York claimants or were liable to be made
subject to such judgments when the New York jurisdiction should be established. In that case the claims
for intervening damages for their occupation of the
property would sweep away all their personal estate
and leave them penniless. No quieting act of the New
York legislature could have saved their homes to these
men because if the New York claimants had acquired a
valid title to those lands no legislative enactment could
take it away from them. Notwithstanding the specious
pretenses of Governor Clinton's proclamation, there
was no safety for those men of Bennington against the
claims of the land jobbers. There was no pretense in
that proclamation of any construction that would save
to Governor Chittenden his property in Williston and
Jericho. Mr. Brownson, the other one of the eight
men named, had a home within the limits of Princetown grant, of which, as we have seen, Mr. Duane was
a large owner. There was nothing in that proclamation
or the resolutions of the New York legislature which
pretended to give protection to the Allens in their

large property interests which have already been described. Of this fact both the Allens had a perfect
appreciation. They knew very well that the re-estab-
lishment of the New York jurisdiction would effect not
only their own utter financial ruin but that of all the
other settlers on the west side of the mountains.

On the other hand they had good reason to believe
that when the matter came properly before the english
tribunals for adjudication the New Hampshire titles
would be sustained. That was the opinion freely
given out by the members of the privy council in
July, 1767. The correspondence of Lord Shelburne,
Lord Hillsborough and Lord Dartmouth already quoted
indicated the same opinion. The report of the board
of trade in 1772 and the action of the privy council
upon it was to the same effect. The Allens were both
perfectly familiar with all these expressions of opinion.
They had made large reference to them in the pamphlets they published in defence of the Vermont claims.
Not only the Allens but in fact all of the Bennington
settlers had the strongest personal interest which anybody could have in the defeat of the New York jurisdiction. That question involved everything which any
of them had in the world.

None of the writers who have discussed the Haldimand negotiations and the conduct of the Vermonters
seem to have appreciated this fact. When learned
men sit in their libraries and write disquisitions on the
duty of good citizens to be patriotic and support the
authorities which control their homes, the situation has
a very different aspect to them from that presented to
citizens who find themselves called on to support
authority which they know will deprive them of any

home and make them exiles and outlaws, and that too in despite of the acknowledged injustice of that procedure. Patriotism consists mainly in the attachment to and the defence of one's home. When that home is unjustly taken from a man there is but little left of patriotic duty. The Vermonters owed nothing to the continental congress. Their applications had uniformly been neglected or refused; and so far as the congress had given any expression of intention up to the time of those Haldimand negotiations, it had been of an intention to sustain the New York jurisdiction.

There can be no doubt that Ethan Allen was entirely sincere when he wrote to the president of congress on the ninth of March that, rather than submit to the jurisdiction of New York, he would retire with the Green Mountain Boys to the mountains and wage continual warfare against their oppressors.

The establishment of British authority over Vermont would have left the condition of the settlers very much like that of the people in the eastern townships of Canada. This condition while not to be preferred to that of the present people of Vermont was one that would give reasonable assurance of protection to private rights. The settlers could not have this assurance under the jurisdiction of New York.

In those days adhesion to the british authority did not necessarily involve the moral turpitude that now attaches to the name of tory. Some of the best men of the settlement were conscientiously in favor of english rule. Mr. James Breakenridge was a worthy citizen and yet he was more than suspected of adhesion to the British claims. There was no more exemplary citizen in the whole extent of the new state than

Jehiel Hawley of Arlington and yet he was an avowed
royalist.

Early in 1781 when the prospects of the colonists
seemed very doubtful there was a decided disposition
on the part of some of the best citizens of New York
to yield the contest with the New Hampshire grants
rather than endanger the interests of the whole country
by the continuation of that dispute. Among these
were General Schuyler and Chancellor Livingston.
Accordingly a resolution was presented to that legislature consenting to the formation of an independent
state of Vermont with the boundary on a line twenty
miles east of the Hudson river. This resolution was
favored by Chancellor Livingston although his family
had been largely interested in those New York grants.
It passed the senate by nearly a unanimous vote;
and on a test vote in the house it appeared that more
than two to one were in favor of its adoption. At
this stage Governor Clinton interfered with the threat
that, unless that measure was abandoned, he would
prorogue the session, as under the constitution he had
power to do. As there was other business of importance for that session, the legislature yielded. From
that time, however, opposition to the state of Vermont
rapidly faded away. That government enforced its
order by vigorous although not very harsh measures
and many of the leading supporters of the New York
interests, like Judge Knowlton of Newfane and Micah
Townsend of Brattleboro, finding further resistance
would be worse than useless, gave their adhesion to the
new state and were from that time among its most
earnest supporters.

The surrender of Lord Cornwallis, in October,

1781, very materially changed the outlook for the
American colonies. From that time the success of the
revolution became assured and the continental congress, being no longer pressed by the fear of a British
diversion in Vermont, was in no haste to fulfill the
promise it had made to the Vermont agents in the
previous August. Complications about the balance of
power between the north and the south began to arise
and at the same time the interest of the claimants of
the Vermont lands under the New York titles again
asserted its influence. At a session of the Vermont
legislature held in October it refused to comply with
the conditions named by congress, but at another
session in the winter following it retracted that refusal
and accepted all the conditions of the resolution of
congress passed August 20th; and the excuse of the
enemies of Vermont was that the new state, having at
first rejected the offer of congress, could not afterwards
by a retraction of that rejection claim anything under
that promise. Whether this was a valid excuse or not
is now immaterial. At all events the continental
congress persisted in its refusal to admit the new state
and passed resolutions threatening to enforce its orders
unless the rulers of the new state yielded.

On November 14, 1781, Governor Chittenden
wrote a long letter to General Washington in relation
to the situation of the state and the causes which had
induced the negotiations with the governor of Canada.
That was a remarkable letter both in respect to what
was stated in it and what was not stated, and, though
not entirely correct in its grammar and not without
fault in its style, it was very adroitly written. Without in terms admitting anything, it justified all that

was claimed and all that was in fact true about those
negotiations. It set forth plainly the defenseless condition of Vermont with its extended frontier on the
lake entirely exposed to invasion by the British forces
in Canada, and stated that it had been abandoned by
congress and that while it was building forts and earth-
works for its own protection the continental officers
had left not even a pick-ax or spade for its use. The
letter proceeds to note the refusal of congress to recognize the new state and claims upon this abandonment
the right to negotiate for its own protection. "

The authorship of this letter has been attributed
to Ira Allen and this is undoubtedly correct. Although
the style of the writings of Ira Allen was less extrava-
gant than that of his brother Ethan, this letter shows
evidence of having been tempered by the cool judgment
of Governor Chittenden. Inasmuch as Ethan Allen
had forwarded the Robinson letters to the president of
congress in March and Governor Chittenden had written to General Washington in November of the same
year and all the proceedings had been so conducted as
to have attracted the attention of the New York
officers as well as those of the continental congress, it
cannot be claimed that there was much concealment
about the Haldimand negotiations.

In the following winter General Washington wrote
a conciliatory reply to Governor Chittenden's letter
advising compliance with the offers of congress and
encouraging the expectation that upon that compliance
the new state would be admitted to the union. The
disposition of congress had however changed.

In December, 1782, congress passed resolutions in
respect to the conduct of the government of the new

state, commanding it to make restitution to some of the New York officials who had been convicted under the state laws for treasonable practices against the Vermont government. In those resolutions congress declared its purpose to enforce compliance with that demand. To those resolutions Governor Chittenden, by direction of his council, forwarded a very prompt and spirited reply, in which he plainly denied the jurisdiction of congress to interfere with the state administration; and, while he did not in terms refuse to obey the mandates of congress, he stated that a question so important ought not to be determined without consideration by the state legislature which was expected to be in session in the following February. This reply was not only forwarded to congress but printed copies were distributed to General Washington and others in the army.

Those resolutions and the evident intention of the Vermonters to disobey them gave General Washington great anxiety, as well it might. He wrote a very plain letter to a personal friend of his in congress calling attention to the situation and to the fact that the attempt to enforce those threats by the use of his army would be very dangerous if not disastrous. In that letter he used this language:

"It is not a trifling force that will subdue them, even supposing they derived no aid from the enemy in Canada. * * The country is very mountainous, full of defiles, and exceedingly strong. The inhabitants for the most part are a hardy race, composed of that kind of people who are best calculated for soldiers; in truth who are soldiers, for many, many hundreds of them are deserters from this army, who having acquired property there would be desperate in defense of it."

This letter further calls attention to the fact that the settlers in Vermont were almost entirely New England men and had the sympathy of New England states and further that his army was mainly composed of soldiers from New England and while he had not dared to take measures to ascertain the actual feeling of the soldiers towards such an enterprise he deemed it unwise to force any issue of that kind. To this letter the general received a reply that he need have no fears that congress would undertake to enforce its threats by the use of his army. The reply further stated that a peculiar state of things produced the act of congress of August, 1781, and a change of circumstances afterwards dictated the delay in coming to a determination on the questions involved.

# CHAPTER XIII.

## AN INCIDENT.

Near the close of the Revolutionary war an incident occurred which, although not strictly within the purpose of this paper, was yet so connected with the principal actors of those times as to have some interest in this connection. This was the attempt by the continental authorities to arrest Colonel Wells of Brattleboro and Judge Knowlton of Newfane for engaging in forwarding correspondence between Governor Haldimand in Canada and Sir Henry Clinton in New York. The Haldimand correspondence shows that it was difficult to get communication between those two departments of the British service. Communication by sailing vessels around north by the way of the St. Lawrence was difficult and liable to be interrupted by privateers. Communication overland was dangerous because the territory to be traversed was largely in control of the continental troops. Beside other agreements made by Ira Allen in those negotiations was one that the new state would permit the transmission of dispatches through its territory. This was expressly stated by him in his history. As we have seen, Colonel Wells of Brattleboro was a personal friend of many of the leading loyalists in New York city and one of the letters in the Haldimand correspondence states that

Colonel Wells had sent his son-in-law to New York
with offers of assistance in conducting that correspondence. Judge Knowlton had been associated with
Colonel Wells in the affairs of Cumberland county
while it was under the New York jurisdiction. He
had adhered to the New York party until it became
evident that there was no use in further adhesion, upon
which he had become interested in the new state and an
officer under its jurisdiction. It is said that in 1780,
while he was in attendance at Philadelphia upon the
continental congress in the interest of New York, he
became acquainted with Ira Allen and a warm personal
friendship had grown up between them which continued during his whole life. Correspondence was for
some time carried on between Canada and New York
with the aid of Knowlton and Wells. Messengers
would come from Canada to Newfane and their mes-
sages would be transferred to Brattleboro where further
messengers were provided by Colonel Wells. Late in
the year 1782 one of the messengers of Colonel Wells
was detected in Rhode Island on his way to New York.
The continental authorities reported the facts to congress and means were taken to secure the arrest of
both Wells and Knowlton. An officer was sent from
Albany with a company or perhaps a detail of men to
go to Brattleboro and make the arrest. When the
officer with his command reached Brattleboro he found
both Wells and Knowlton had escaped. It has since
transpired, and was stated by Ira Allen in his history,
that Colonel Wells having notice of what was going on
had started for the british lines. This was in January,
1783. On his journey he stopped for the night in the
mountains at the place of Captain Otley in Bromley,

now Peru.   While he was at supper the captain with
the force from Albany that had been sent for his
capture stopped at the same place.   The captain made
no secret of his errand but as we may be assured Wells
did not disclose his identity.   He waited until morning
when the loud-mouthed captain had departed and then
found his way to the house of Ethan Allen in Sunderland   He was aided by the Allens in his escape.
When it became known that Knowlton and Wells had
escaped there was great commotion in the continental
congress and one of its members was accused of having
forwarded information to them of their intended arrest.
The man so accused was Dr. Arnold, member from
Rhode Island.   He denied it and no evidence was
produced against him.   He was, however, well known
to be friendly to the new state, both in congress
and out of it.   Shortly after the war he came to
Vermont and became the founder of what is now the
town of St. Johnsbury.   Very early he became a
member of the Vermont council and for several years
his name appears in the rolls of that body next to that
of Luke Knowlton of Newfane.   There was, however,
no great reason to suspect anybody of giving clandes-
tine information of the proceedings which resulted in
the attempt to arrest those men.   The whole affair was
managed in a very bungling manner.

   This was of itself sufficient to give warning to men
much less acute than either Wells or Knowlton were
that it was time for them to retire.   They remained
within the british lines until the conclusion of peace in
the following summer.   For their six or eight months
banishment they both managed to get from England
a very handsome compensation.   In fact it was pecun-

iarily about the best year's work either of them ever did. Wells got a grant of land in the eastern townships of Canada sufficient to give 1200 acres to each of his eleven children, and it was located on some of the best lands in the townships. Knowlton got a grant of probably an equal amount of land, which is still held by descendants bearing his name. In the county of Brome in Canada the little hamlet which is the county seat still bears the name of Knowlton. In that village the principal house, an establishment of manorial character, is or was a few years ago still held by the descendants of Luke Knowlton, who held high position among their neighbors and in the provincial government.

It is interesting to note the history of that man. He was the most adroit man in the whole history of the new state. In 1772 he was interested in the New Hampshire grant of Newfane. Before he put himself within the power of the New York government by making settlements or spending his money on improvements he went to New York and made application for a confirmatory charter. He reached New York in the winter following the failure of Sheriff Ten Eyck with his great posse from Albany to get possession of the Bennington lands, just at the time when Ethan Allen and his Green Mountain Boys were at the height of their defiance of the New York authorities and doing lawless acts which Governor Tryon was utterly powerless to prevent. At that time no speculator could be found with hardihood enough to purchase a claim against the settlers on the New Hampshire grants, and Governor Tryon was forced either to lose his fees entirely or accept such terms as were offered him. Mr.

Knowlton was altogether too bright a man not to be aware of the situation and he was not bashful in availing himself of it. He got his new charter and in it he secured all of the franchises in the New Hampshire charter; in fact it was a copy of Governor Wentworth's charter. It gave the settlers all the advantages they had before, including the New England town meeting and the small quit rent. He undoubtedly was able to secure a very considerable reduction from the usual fees for such re-charters, but naturally, if such reduction was made, the provincial authorities would be very careful that it should not appear upon the records.

Knowlton himself settled in Newfane. At its organization he was made the town clerk, and for fifty-nine out of sixty following years either he or some member of his family was continued in that office. In the organization of Cumberland county he was counted as an adherent of the existing government, but took no very prominent part in its management. He was a member of the Cumberland council of safety for a year or two; was sent in 1780 to Philadelphia to present the claims of the New York authorities to the continental congress. While he was there he became acquainted with Ira Allen, who represented the state government of Vermont, and a personal friendship sprung up between them which was never broken. When it became apparent that the New York claims were only maintained by a small minority of the state and the obstinacy of the governor, he gave his adhesion to the state government. He had during Governor Tryon's administration received a grant of five thousand acres of land in Franklin county, near the town of Fletcher, as it is described. When he was obliged to leave the state in January, 1783, the records of the governor and council show that a person was appointed justice of the peace in Windom county in place of Knowlton, who had left the state. The town records show that another man was elected town clerk in his place. In 1784 he was re-elected and also elected to the Vermont legislature. They show that he took a very prominent part in the legislature and was a member of some of the most important committees. Within a year or two he was elected a member of the council and judge of the supreme court of the state for one year. He was for many years chief judge of the court for Windom county. When the controversy between New York and Vermont was finally adjusted by the payment of $30,000 by Vermont for the satisfaction of the New York claims he got his dividend on the five thousand acres of land in Franklin county.

He got through the governor and council of Vermont a grant of ten thousand acres of land under the name of Knowlton's Gore, probably covering his New York grant, for which he paid the usual fee of 130 pounds and 19 shillings. He sold that land within a month to Joseph Baker for 500 pounds lawful money, and upon his own motion in the council the name was changed from Knowlton's Gore to Bakersfield, which is still retained. It was no ordinary man that had the address to obtain land grants from three hostile governments; and yet during all these transactions he retained the confidence of his neighbors, and there was no imputation upon his integrity. His descendants have occupied high positions not only in Canada but in the United States.

A grandson of Judge Knowlton still survives in Windham county.    He has held the highest offices of his state and has well deserved its highest honors. He is the last survivor of the war governors of Vermont and many sons of that state have a kindly respect for Frederick Holbrook.

# CHAPTER XIV.

## AN INDEPENDENT SOVEREIGNTY.

The close of the Revolutionary war found the new state of Vermont in the exercise of all the functions of an independent sovereignty. It employed organized forces to defend the state against foreign invasion and to enforce the judgments of its courts against such of its settlers as refused to respect its jurisdiction. It appropriated the public lands within its borders and sold them for the benefit of the state. It raised other revenues by the sale of lands confiscated from the enemies of the government as well as by taxation in the ordinary course. It had established courts of justice and enforced their mandates by the aid of military power, when necessary. It established a postoffice department with mail routes and postoffices. It conducted negotiations with foreign countries. Very soon after the close of the war it provided for the coinage of money. By legislation it adopted a code of laws, making provision for the enforcement of contracts and original provisions for relief against the harsh doctrines of common law liabilities.

During the latter part of the Revolutionary war the new state had attracted the attention of settlers and its population had grown very steadily. In 1771 n enumeration was had of the inhabitants on the east side of the mountains. From that census and an estimate of the population on the west side the whole number of inhabitants was about 7,000. From estimates made in 1781 that population had increased to about 30,000. By the enumeration of 1791 it was shown that the population had increased to between 85,000 and 86,000.

Among the causes for this rapid increase of inhabitants was the vigor of the state administration, which gave ample assurance for the protection of private rights. Another cause was the light burdens of taxation. The affairs of the state were managed with great economy and the revenues from the sales of land were nearly sufficient to pay the whole expenses. While the neighboring states were laboring under heavy burdens of debt caused by the Revolutionary war, Vermont had, by the refusal of congress to recognize the new state, become exempt from any of those burdens. On this account after the close of the war the new state was not at all anxious for admission into the confederacy. After the disbandment of the continental army there was no ground for fearing any attempt by New York to enforce its jurisdiction. In fact the Vermont settlers continued to have the sympathy of the people of New York.

The growth of the new state had opened fields for men of the learned professions. Among those who came soon after the establishment of the new state government were two Connecticut men, who were destined to become very important factors in the establishment of the civil polity of the state. These men were Stephen Row Bradley, who settled at Westminster in 1779, and Nathaniel Chipman, who about the same

time came to Tinmouth. Both these men were gradu-
ates of Yale College, Bradley in the class of 1775 and
Chipman two years later. They were both lawyers
educated for the bar in Connecticut and both at once
took high rank in their profession. Mr. Bradley was
made colonel of a militia regiment and afterwards
brigadier general; and after the organization of the
state government he was for fourteen years one of its
senators in congress. Mr. Chipman was judge of the
supreme court, United States senator and chief justice
of the supreme court of the state. He was the most
active man in procuring the adjustment of the difficulties with New York and, on that account, has
in this paper been included among the four men
from Salisbury who had the most to do with the
establishment of the new state. Another man educated for the same profession was Micah Townsend
of Brattleboro. He was a native of Long Island
and was educated at Princeton, where he graduated
in 1766. He was then admitted to the bar of the
state of New York, where he continued in his
practice until the breaking out of the Revolutionary
war in which he served for a time. He located at
Brattleboro and married a daughter of Colonel Wells.
There he naturally at once took sides with the New
York party in Cumberland county until about 1780
when, finding that further resistance to the new state
government would be worse than useless, he accepted
the situation as he found it and became a useful member of the Vermont government. There were other
lawyers among the new settlers in Vermont. Most of
these had come from Connecticut. Judge Chipman
and Mr. Townsend were appointed commissioners to

revise the statutes of the new state. As the leading lawyers and a large portion of the inhabitants of the state were from Connecticut it was very natural that the statutes of Vermont should be largely copied from those of that state. By this legislation prominence was given to the township organization as the unit of municipal corporations as distinguished from the county organizations of some other states. The New England town meeting was preserved with all its characteristics.

During this period was enacted a statute which was then a novelty in English and American legislation, but which has since been copied in different forms by many of the states in the Union and is now recognized as eminently just and a necessary amelioration of the common law. That was the statute which was and still is known in Vermont as the "betterment act" and in some other states is now designated as the "occupying claimants" law. By the common law in all actions of ejectment the prevailing party recovered the lands in dispute with all the improvements made upon them by the defendant without regard to any question of the justice or the injustice of the forfeiture of such improvements. The case of the Bennington settlers furnished a very marked illustration of the injustice of that rule. Those settlers had bought their lands of the king through his agent, who at the time of that purchase had possession and control of the lands conveyed. At the time of their purchase they had no reason to question the authority of the agents of the king to make the conveyances under which they held. Relying upon these grants purporting to come from the sovereign authority these settlers had improved their lands and most of them had invested their all in these new homes. The greed with which the New York speculators had sought grants of these improved lands for the sake of the profits to be got by the forfeiture of those improvements was a very notable feature in that contest. In the early history of the state there had been, in the absence of any system of registry of deeds, numerous instances of purchase by settlers who had been deceived in the character of the titles they got. These unjust results attracted the attention of Governor Chittenden and through his exertions was procured the enactment of the laws in consideration. The first of these was passed in 1781. In 1784 a revision was made of these laws and the form of relief to be given by them was submitted to a committee of which Mr. Bradley and Mr. Chipman were members; and the result was that in 1785 a law was enacted which has been in substance retained to this day and has become the precedent for similar enactments in most of the other states of the Union. The substance of that law is that where the purchasers of lands have in good faith and relying upon the title they bought improved the property they purchased, they cannot be ejected without allowance of compensation for the increased value of the lands occasioned by those improvements. The rulers of that new state are entitled to the credit of being the originators of this very necessary legislation.

During the same period the courts of the state made a departure from the usual rules in the matter of tax titles, which in later years they were forced to retract, and the result was that large tracts of lands passed on tax sales which would not now be considered regular. Among those sales were most of the townships of

Georgia and Swanton, which had been purchased by
Levi Allen. This man was the brother of Ethan and
Ira Allen, but had been a tory during the Revolutionary
war. Confiscation proceedings had been commenced
against him at the instance of his brother Ira. After
the close of the war tax titles were taken to these lands
by Ira Allen. As those tax deeds were witnessed by
Nathaniel Chipman and Levi Allen himself, it would
seem that the principal purpose of those tax sales was
to relieve the lands of the cloud upon the title caused
by the confiscation proceedings. Among those tax
titles it is said there were several which cut off some of
Governor Wentworth's claims to the five hundred acre
tracts he had reserved to himself as "governor's rights"
in the New Hampshire charters.

The history of those later times is largely taken
up with an account of the forlorn resistance made to the
state government by the adherents of New York residing mainly in the townships of Guilford, Halifax and
Marlboro, which was finally overcome in the winter of
1784. Among those who experienced the severest
effects of that resistance was Charles Phelps, of Marlboro, a man in whose character was found the strangest
compound of both the heroic and ridiculous elements.
That story has, however, little to do with the dispute
between the settlers and the New York claimants.

## CHAPTER XV.

### FINAL SETTLEMENT WITH NEW YORK.

In October, 1789, there had come the twentieth anniversary of the commencement of forcible resistance to the New York speculators by the Vermont settlers.. During these twenty years great changes had been wrought. The New Hampshire grants had increased in population more than tenfold. A now nation was being formed in the place of the colonies which during that interval had asserted and established their independence of the British crown. A new state had been formed by the people of these New Hampshire grants.

During this period many of the prominent actors in the contest had passed away. Ethan Allen had died in the winter previous. Heman Allen had died of a decline caused by his exposure in the battle of Bennington. Remember Baker had been killed in one of the first engagements of the Revolutionary war. Zimri Allen had also died; and of all the members of the Onion River Company Ira Allen was the only survivor. Seth Warner after an honorable service in the war had with broken health returned to the home of his boyhood, where he, too, had died in 1784. The men of Bennington who had commenced that contest had many of them passed away. The Rev. Jedediah Dewey, their pastor and leader, had died in 1778. Robert

Cochran had removed from the state. Of the men on the other side of this contest death had claimed a large number. Governor Colden had died early in the Revolutionary war. Crean Brush and Colonel Wells, who had been the members from Cumberland county of the New York assembly which had passed those notable acts of outlawry, were both dead. Attorney-General Kempe had been banished and his estate confiscated because he was a tory. Governors Dunmore and Tryon had been driven out of the country. Of the men who had manifested the most bitterness against the resistance of the settlers, Governor Clinton, who had been chairman of the committee to make the report upon which were based those acts of outlawry, still survived and was unrelenting in his bitterness. Of the men who had sought to make their fortunes by appropriating the farms of the settlers, Mr. Duane was still the leader, although he had recently been induced to turn over the active management of his claims to a younger man.

During that month of October, 1789, there had come to the legislature of Vermont overtures for the settlement of this long subsisting controversy. Those overtures had come from the legislature of New York. In the change those twenty years had wrought it had come to pass that New York was more anxious for this settlement than was Vermont. It was time for a settlement. The best men of the country were then organizing a national government. The continuance of the contest between New York and Vermont was a very serious obstacle in the way of the development of the new nation. Of this fact the best men in New York were becoming more and more convinced. Such

men were Alexander Hamilton, John Jay, Chancellor
Livingston and General Schuyler.  The only thing in
the way of that settlement was the interest of the New
York claimants to the Vermont lands.  Even those
claimants had come to appreciate, what so many speculators have found to be true, that, in the language
of the late Daniel Drew, "speculation is a rosky
business."

This suspicion of the uncertainties of speculation
must have been very much intensified by the result of
the action of the state of Massachusetts against New
York, which had been brought in the federal court in
1784 for the recovery of lands claimed by Massachusetts under its royal charter.  To this action the state
of New York had made its answer and Mr. Duane had
been employed as its counsel and had filed an elaborate
brief which is set forth in the collections of the New
York Historical Society.  The defence against this
claim of Massachusetts rested on substantially the same
grounds as the claim to the territory of the New
Hampshire grants.  Indeed were it not for the fact
that in those collections it is stated that this brief was
used against the claim of Massachusetts it might easily
have been supposed that the paper there published was
one of the numerous papers Mr. Duane had filed in the
Vermont controversy.  His claim was based upon the
allegations of the Dutch claim to the Connecticut river
as its eastern boundary and the St. Lawrence as the
northern boundary of the dutch province of New York
upon the grants of Charles II to his brother the Duke
of York.  From those papers it appears that General
Hamilton was associated with Mr. Duane as counsel.
It is easy to imagine how unsatisfactory were these

grounds of defense to a good lawyer like General
Hamilton. The claim of dutch occupancy had no support in fact and the claim of title under the grant to
the Duke of York which had become "merged" but
was still subsisting must have been incomprehensible.
At all events the authorities of New York after full
consideration of Mr. Duane's defense deemed it unwise
to rest their case upon it and so made haste to settle
the adverse claim. In that settlement they conceded to
Massachusetts nearly six million of acres of the best
lands in the state, which was then the largest recovery
in any action that had ever been brought in America.
If that defense was not good as against the Massachusetts claim, which had no equities in its support,
the speculators might naturally infer that it would be
at least doubtful as against the claims of the Vermont
settlers, especially as in the latter case it had been
expressly conceded that all the equities were in favor
of the settlers.

In the winter of 1782 the legislature of New York
passed an act which by its terms did all that any legislative enactment could do to confirm all the New Hampshire charters. By that enactment the titles of all the
settlers in the state, except those whose lands were
covered by the New York grants were fully confirmed.
It would not be a confirmation of the title to the township of Hinsdale, but that title was good without confirmation and must have been so held even by the New
York courts. Had that action been taken ten years
earlier it would have had some effect. It very likely
would have prevented the creation of the new state and
perhaps would have postponed, although no human
power could have prevented, the American Revolution.

Coming at the time it did this action of the New York
legislature made no impression even upon the "woods
people." The people of Cumberland county who
would have been most benefited by that confirmation
had by the "politic measures" of the new state become
too much interested in land grants from that state to
be willing to favor the New York jurisdiction. In
1787 the attorney of the New York claimants com-
plained that the settlers had taken no notice of this
legislation.

Numerous attempts were made in the New York
assembly to procure the consent of that state to the
independence of Vermont and its admission to the
continental union. In 1787 a bill to that effect was
pending before the legislature. To this bill the land
claimants objected and appeared by their attorney,
Richard Harrison, and had a hearing before the assembly. The arguments of that counsel and the speech
of General Hamilton in reply are preserved among the
Hamilton papers. Mr. Harrison's argument was not
based upon the stereotyped claims of Mr. Duane about
the grant to the Duke of York and the extent of the
dutch province. It is evident that the claimants
had become doubtful of the strength of those arguments. His claim was based upon the state constitution
of New York which had declared the New Hampshire
grants to be included within that state. He objected
to the acknowledgment of the independence of Vermont because it would deprive his clients of their
property. In this respect his argument was not sound
because the independence of Vermont would only affect
the tribunal before which they should seek their
remedy and not the rights they claimed. It had been

urged that by the confederation a tribunal had been
provided for in the federal court named in that confederation.  To this Mr. Harrison objected that it was
doubtful whether such court would have jurisdiction
and urged especially that its proceedings were too
expensive to be invoked by any private citizens.  This
came with ill grace from the representative of Mr.
Duane who, in 1774, had found fault with the Vermont
settlers because they had made forcible resistance
instead of taking an appeal to the privy council of
England.  That privy council was the most expensive
tribunal on earth and a fee of a thousand guineas was
the ordinary compensation of lawyers who would naturally be entrusted with such cases.  General Hamilton
made a very pertinent reply to this question of expense
by stating that it would be much cheaper to try the
rights of those claimants in the federal court than it
would be to undertake to conquer Vermont by military
force.   In fact the real objection of the claimants to a
federal court was that they had become very much
convinced that the federal court would decide against
them on the validity of the New Hampshire titles.  Mr.
Harrison's argument contains a paragraph which undoubtedly expressed the real feeling of his clients :

"In the present situation of things, whilst the
independence of Vermont is not acknowledged by this
state while some of the inhabitants of that district
have their hopes and others their apprehensions that
they may again be reduced to the obedience which they
owe this government, many, if not all, of them, are
solicitous to secure a good and permanent title for their
possession by purchasing from the petitioners their
rights under the state of New York."

This was undoubtedly the real policy of the New

York speculators,—to keep the question of titles so unsettled that the people of Vermont could by a kind of blackmailing process be forced to pay something for the extinguishment of those claims. The reply of General Hamilton to this position was a plain statement of the situation as it then existed. He stated that Vermont was in fact severed from New York and had been so for years; that there was no reasonable prospect of recovering possession of it and the attempt to accomplish that recovery would be attended with certain and serious consequences.

It is to be remembered that New York was not then the "Empire" state it now is. Mr. Hamilton stated that the population of New York was not much more than double that of Vermont; that there was a great difference between a defensive and an offensive campaign where the defense was aided by the natural strength of the country. Mr. Hamilton further stated:

"No assistance is to be expected from our neighbors. Their opinion of the origin of the controversy between this state and the people of Vermont whether well or ill founded is not generally in our favor."

The arguments of General Hamilton prevailed before the assembly but the objectors managed to kill the bill in the senate. Two years later a similar bill was presented upon petition of John Jay and numerous other well known citizens of New York, many of whom were interested as claimants under the New York grants of the Vermont lands. That bill passed the assembly by a vote of 40 to 11, but was again defeated in the senate.

In the meantime the people of Vermont were still pursuing their "politic measures" to increase their

strength by the use of their land grants. They had
granted to John Jay fourteen thousand acres in the
township which still bears his name. They granted to
Samuel Avery several tracts of land which are still
designated as Avery's Gores and other lands now a
part of the township of Troy. They had granted to
John Kelly the township of Kellyvale, now Lowell.
They had made grants in which it appears that Governor Clinton himself was interested. They had also
granted the town of Johnson to a company of which
William Samuel Johnson was a member. Mr. Johnson
was a relative of Governor Chittenden. His father
had been president of Columbia College, a position
which he himself afterwards occupied. He had been
the agent of Connecticut, and, as has already been seen,
had rendered great assistance to Captain Robinson in
his application to the privy council.

While these politic measures had undoubtedly
produced a very strong effect in strengthening the
position of the new state, they had been opposed by
some, among whom was Judge Chipman. In 1780, at
the time of the adoption of the policy of granting
lands, the legislature upon the report of a committee
to consider that question adopted a resolution indicating
that any grants of the New York government after the
prohibition of the king forbidding such grants should
be considered as objections to new grants of the same
lands to even deserving applicants. This conclusion
was undoubtedly correct because the title of the lands
being in the king all charters and conveyances of those
lands must be made in the name of the king by his
agents. Upon the elementary principles of the law of
agency after the revocation of authority no valid con-

veyances can be made by such agents, but at that time
it seemed to be a strange thing that the proprietary
title of public lands should be held by any other
authority than that having legislative jurisdiction over
the same territory. Accordingly the determination
that the state of Massachusetts owned lands within the
territory of New York was a novelty, and so was the
conclusion that the state of Connecticut owned lands
within the Western Reserve in Ohio. In our time
such titles held by the United States government are
very familiar and the investigation of questions arising
out of such proprietary ownership are matters of daily
experience to lawyers in the western states. Even
Judge Chipman failed to appreciate this particular
feature of the law, and in a letter to Alexander Hamilton admitted that it was the general understanding
that where the Vermont grants of lands conflicted with
prior grants under the New York authority the title of
the New York grants would be sustained. In the case
of Jacob vs. Smead his ruling was to the effect that
while the title under the New Hampshire charter was
good, still after the surrender of that charter a good
title came from the regrant by the government of New
York. Mr. B. H. Hall speaks of Judge Chipman's
opinion that the New York title would be preferred to
the Vermont title as if it referred to the title under the
New Hampshire charters. This is incorrect, as will be
seen from a careful examination of Judge Chipman's
letter and from his opinion in the case referred to.
Holding this opinion Judge Chipman was naturally
very anxious to procure an adjustment of the difficulty
and so took the initiative in opening a correspondence
with General Hamilton which led to the final settle-

ment. The result was, that in the summer of 1789 a bill was passed by the New York legislature proposing the appointment of commissioners to meet other commissioners to be selected by Vermont to agree on the terms of a settlement; and at the October session of the Vermont legislature of the same year a copy of this bill was presented to the Vermont legislature which was met by the passage of a similar bill appointing on the part of Vermont Isaac Tichenor, Stephen R. Bradley, Nathaniel Chipman, Elijah Paine, Ira Allen, Stephen Jacob, and Israel Smith, commissioners on the part of Vermont. This bill was sent by the house of representatives to the governor and council for their concurrence on the 19th of October, 1789, the anniversary of the date of the first forcible resistance to the New York claims. After the usual amount of preliminary negotiations it was finally agreed that if the state of Vermont would pay $30,000 on or before the first day of June, 1794,

"All rights and titles to lands within the state of Vermont under grants from the late colony of New York or from the state of New York, should cease."

The only grants excepted were such as had been made in confirmation of former grants under New Hampshire. This action of the commissioners of the two states was ratified by the legislatures; and the money was paid and accepted by the claimants.

None of the claimants to those lands ever attempted to assert any title as against this settlement. If their titles had been good they had the undoubted right to have their claims tried either in the state courts of Vermont or in the United States courts, but none of these claimants ever chose to do so. Conse-

quently this contest of twenty years' duration was
finally settled.

Steps were at once taken for the admission of the
new state into the Union; and on the 16th of February, 1791, an act was passed by congress providing
that on the 4th of March following "the said state, by
the name and style of the State of Vermont, shall be
received into this union as a new and entire member of
the United States of America."

# CHAPTER XVI.

## CONCLUSION.

The long contest between the settlers and the speculators resulted in a victory for the settlers and in the establishment of a new state. Now after a lapse of more than a hundred years there are still many people, not only in Vermont but elsewhere, who are glad of this result and are proud of that victory.

The credit for this fortunate result must be given, in the first instance, to the men of Bennington who commenced that contest against great odds. They were not aggressors. They simply insisted on holding what was their own both in law and in justice, and their resistance was to what they deemed the unjust decisions of the authorities set over them. Not least among these men of Bennington must be counted the sturdy pastor of their church. When the people of Vermont shall learn fully to appreciate the men to whom they are indebted for the independence of their state they will come to respect the memory of the Reverend Jedediah Dewey.

The men of Bennington, however, could not have prevailed in their contest without the assistance of other men. They needed a bold and resolute leader. Such a man they found in Ethan Allen. He was not only a bold and valiant champion in the fight but a

vigorous and successful advocate of the settlers with
his pen. He wrote and published numerous articles
defending them against the claims of Mr. Duane and
his associates and it cannot be denied that his arguments have stood the test of time better than those of
more learned men. His style was objected to as being
unpolished and rough. His composition showed, however, that he had something to say and that that something was exactly pertinent to the subject of his
writing, and he managed to express his ideas in clear
and forcible language. With these merits the defects
of his style may be easily forgiven.

There was another man without whom the state of
Vermont could not have maintained its existence.
That man was Thomas Chittenden, the first governor.
He too was one of the men from Salisbury. Born in
Guilford, Connecticut, in 1730, his family moved to
Salisbury in his childhood, and upon arriving at man-
hood he became a leading inhabitant of the town,
representing it in the colonial assembly for several
years and being advanced to the position of colonel in
the state militia. When he was forty-four years of
age he moved to Williston where he became the owner
of extensive tracts of valuable land. With the possible
exception of Dr. Arnold of St. Johnsbury, it is probable that he brought more property into the state than
any other of its early settlers. Although uncultivated
and with very meagre education and small knowledge
of books, he naturally had a strong mind and good judgment and possessed the faculty of discovering the
merits of questions presented to him without being
embarrassed by technical rules. He was for nearly
twenty years the governor of the state, and was wise and

prudent in his administration. Without his wise counsels, which served as regulators to the energy of the Allens, it is not at all probable that the state could have overcome the opposition it encountered.

Another of the men from Salisbury was Ira Allen. He early became interested in the state organization, and to his fertility of resources and skill the new state was many times indebted for its extrication from difficulties that seemed insurmountable. He was the originator of most of the measures taken by the state to strengthen its position. While it cannot be denied that some of the measures dictated by his policy were more acute than wise, he was in the main successful. He too was a writer. His papers, as they have been preserved, show rare skill and force for a man of his age and opportunities for culture. He had a faculty of saying well what was best to be said, and that other equally rare faculty of not saying whatever the circumstances of the case required to be left unsaid. A measure of the capacity of Ira Allen as a writer can be found by a comparison of his writings with those of General Bradley. These men were nearly of the same age. Both employed their pens in defense of the new state. Bradley had the benefit of the best culture the times afforded. He was a graduate of Yale College and studied law under Tapping Reeve, who was then the best tutor for young lawyers in the country and who has hardly been excelled in later times. General Bradley was a man of natural power of intellect and, while in the United States senate, he was a leader of the party that supported the democratic administration and among the foremost, if not the foremost, member of that senate. Ira Allen had few advantages of early

education. He was graduated in the woods as a surveyor, in which employment he had entered while a
boy in his teens. Yet his writings compare very
favorably with those of his associate who was more
favored in education and culture. Most assuredly the
state of Vermont owes its existence to the labors of
Ira Allen, and the story of the misfortunes of his
later years cannot fail to awaken the sympathy of the
friends of that state.

There was another man from Salisbury, and he
was born there. That man was Nathaniel Chipman, a
little younger than Ira Allen and a little older than
General Bradley. After serving in the continental
army he came to Vermont and, as has been seen, was
largely instrumental in bringing about the final settlement with New York. While it can in no sense be
said that the state owes its existence to Judge Chipman,
it is true that his labors hastened the settlement of its
difficulties and its final establishment as a member of
the Union.

Of these four men the little town of Salisbury has
reason to be proud. That town and the county of
Litchfield furnished other men who gained well deserved fame by their valuable services to the new state.

So far as the establishment of the new state
effected a separation from New York it undoubtedly
promoted the best interests of all concerned. The
settlers of Vermont were almost exclusively New England people imbued with the purely democratic pecul-
iarities of that section. They were a people among
whom "the hired man" was the peer of his employer.
They knew no aristocracy except such as a man was able
to earn for himself. There was great contrast between

the manners of these people and those of the people of
New York. Governor Colden in the extract quoted in the
first part of this article very clearly stated the difference
between these two communities.   To illustrate this distinction we need only to recall the two governors of the
new states.   Governor Chittenden was a plain man who
kept a country tavern and with his own hands performed the most menial services of his farm.   Governor
Clinton was a man of fortune, of family, an aristocrat
by birth and by practice.

   To have forced a political union of such divergent
elements would have been a continual source of bicker-
ings and contention.   There was at that time no love
among the New Yorkers for the yankees.   This dislike
is apparent in the literature of New York during the
period next following the adjustment of these difficulties.   That dislike is very manifest in the writings
of that heartiest of haters, Fennimore Cooper, and crops
out even in those of the genial Washington Irving.

   At first it would seem to be a matter of regret
that the two states of New Hampshire and Vermont
were separated.   For many reasons one strong state
would have seemed preferable to two small ones.   Still,
there is a larger sense in which the separation of
Vermont and New Hampshire was not a matter of
regret but of congratulation.   By that separation and
out of the contest which ensued, there was brought
about among the Vermont settlers a development of
character and a discipline which has given to the
people of that little state a standing of which they
and their descendants are justly proud.   That resolute
energy and fearless assertion of their own rights which
was developed in that contest, has brought forth fruits

in the present times, and from that development has come that which makes us, her sons, whether at home or in distant lands, most glad to remember that we are still Green Mountain Boys.

www.ingramcontent.com/pod-product-compliance
Lightning Source LLC
Chambersburg PA
CBHW030843270326
41928CB00007B/1195